GOOD HOUSEKEEPING

MICROWAVE

Fish

COOKBOOK

For the best results in half the time

GOOD HOUSEKEEPING

MICROWAVE Fish COOKBOOK

For the best results in half the time

Janet Smith

EBURY PRESS, LONDON

Published by Ebury Press
Division of The National Magazine Company Limited
Colquhoun House
27–37 Broadwick Street
London W1V 1FR

First Impression 1987

ISBN 0 85223 686 7 (Hardback)
0 85223 681 6 (Paperback)

Senior Editor: Fiona MacIntyre
Editor: Felicity Jackson
Designer: Grahame Dudley Design
Photography: James Murphy
Stylist: Cathy Sinker
Cover photograph: Mixed Fish Salad (page 96)

Computerset in Great Britain by MFK Typesetting Ltd, Hitchin, Herts
Printed in Great Britain at The Bath Press, Bath, Avon

CONTENTS

▪ *General Recipe Notes* ▪

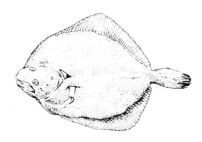

Follow either metric or imperial measures for the recipes in this book; they are not interchangeable.

Bowl Sizes

Small bowl = about 900 ml (1½ pints)
Medium bowl = about 2.3 litres (4 pints)
Large bowl = about 3.4 litres (6 pints)
Large shallow dish = about 1.7 litres (3 pints) (12 inches) round
All recipes in this book were tested using the stated weight of fish. Because of variations in fish sizes, it may not always be possible to buy fish of a corresponding weight. Buy fish of a similar weight and either increase or decrease the cooking time as appropriate (see chart on page 14 and notes on cooking fish on page 13).

Covering

Cook uncovered, unless otherwise stated.
At the time of going to press, it has been recommended by the Ministry of Agriculture, Fisheries and Food that the use of cling film should be avoided in microwave cooking. When a recipe requires you to cover the container, cover with either a lid or a plate, leaving a gap to let steam escape.

Understanding Power Output and Cooker Settings

Unlike conventional ovens, the power output and heat controls on various microwave cookers do not follow a standard formula. When manufacturers refer to a 700-watt cooker, they are referring to the cooker's POWER OUTPUT: its INPUT, which is indicated on the back of the cooker, is double that figure. The higher the wattage of a cooker, the faster the rate of cooking, thus food cooked at 700 watts on full power cooks in half the time of food cooked at 350 watts. That said, the actual cooking performance of one 700-watt cooker may vary slightly from another with the same wattage because factors such as cooker cavity size affect cooking performance. The vast majority of microwave cookers sold today are either 600, 650 or 700 watt cookers, but there are many cookers still in use which may be 400 and 500 watts.

In this book
HIGH refers to 100% full power output of 600–700 watts.
MEDIUM refers to 60% of full power.
LOW is 35% of full power.

Whatever the wattage of your cooker, the HIGH/FULL setting will always be 100% of the cooker's output. Thus your highest setting will correspond to HIGH.

However, the MEDIUM and LOW settings used in this book may not be equivalent to the MEDIUM and LOW settings marked on your cooker. As these settings vary according to power input, we have included the following calculation so you can estimate the correct setting for your cooker. This simple calculation should be done before you use the recipes for the first time, to ensure successful results. Multiply the percentage power required by the total number of settings on your cooker and divide by 100. To work out what setting MEDIUM and LOW correspond to on your cooker, follow the same guide lines, i.e.

MEDIUM (60%)

$$= \frac{\% \text{ Power}}{\text{required}} \times \frac{\text{Total number}}{\text{of cooker settings}} \div 100$$

= Correct setting

$$= \frac{60 \times 9}{100} = 5$$

LOW (35%)

$$= \frac{\% \text{ Power}}{\text{required}} \times \frac{\text{Total number}}{\text{of cooker settings}} \div 100$$

= Correct setting

$$= \frac{35 \times 9}{100} = 3$$

If your cooker power output is lower than 600 watts, then you must allow a longer cooking and thawing time for all recipes and charts in this book.

Add approximately 10–15 seconds per minute for a 600 watt cooker, and 15–20 seconds per minute for a 500 watt cooker.

COMBINED COOKERS

Combined cookers combine conventional and microwave methods of cooking so that food browns as well as cooking quickly. If you own a combined cooker, follow your manufacturer's instructions on the technique of browning or crisping a dish.

· INTRODUCTION ·

THE CURRENT *desire for a healthier diet means that fish is gaining in popularity. Fish has both a low saturated fat content and a low calorie content; it's a cheaper source of protein than meat and it can be prepared in just as wide a range of ways, especially in the microwave.*

But for some reason, many people have an aversion to fresh fish, thinking it difficult and time-consuming to prepare. However, if you follow the instructions on page 10, you will be amazed just how quickly and easily fresh fish can be prepared. But if you really cannot face preparing a whole, raw fish, ask your fishmonger to do it for you – for most, this is a normal part of the service.

Once prepared, you'll see just how easy it is to make delicious dishes after only a few minutes cooking time – fish isn't a dense food, so the cooking times are naturally short. Because of this, it retains its nutrients, and has a lovely moist texture.

Fish is such a versatile food, that it can be used in a wide variety of recipes. I've included a selection ranging from breakfasts and brunch through main, light and cold dishes to classic dishes of the world. Indeed, the inspiration for many of the dishes in this book comes from the cuisines of other countries where fish has always been rated highly. For example, Indonesian soup (see page 29) is based on a classic Indonesian recipe and uses the delicate flavouring of tamarind and lemon grass to make a delicious main course soup with scampi, squid and coconut milk. While Fish with Coriander Masala (see page 75) is a strongly flavoured Indian dish consisting of a spicy tomato and coriander sauce poured over the whole fish and cooked in only 30 minutes.

The range of fish actually used in the recipes is also broad – from the ever-popular cod, haddock plaice to the more exotic swordfish, tuna, red mullet and langoustine. These may not be available at all times in your area, so I've given alternatives wherever possible. If you are ever in doubt, however, always ask your fishmonger's advice.

I do hope this book will inspire you, and prove that cooking fish with the help of your microwave is a quick, easy and pleasurable experience not to be missed.

BUYING FRESH FISH AND SHELLFISH

Always buy fish from a reputable fishmonger who has a quick turnover and gets supplies daily.

Whole fish should have clear, bright eyes, bright red or pink gills, shiny firm, not limp, bodies and firmly attached scales. Fillets, steaks and cutlets should be white and translucent and not show signs of dryness or discoloration, nor should they be wet and slimy. All fresh fish should smell of the sea – do not buy any that smells strongly of fish or smells unpleasant.

Shellfish should be very fresh as they are more perishable than any other fish. They too, should have a clean sea smell and clear fresh colour – avoid any that are dull looking. Look for tightly closed and undamaged shells.

SEASONAL AVAILABILITY OF FISH AND SHELLFISH

Many fish are now available throughout the year, but are at their best during certain months. The chart below gives an indication of availability, but it also depends on where you live and the weather conditions. Most recipes in this book suggest several suitable fish for each dish.

FISH	SEASON	FISH	SEASON
Bass	AUGUST–MARCH	Mullet	
Bream (sea)	JUNE–FEBRUARY	– Red	MAY–NOVEMBER
Brill	JUNE–FEBRUARY	– Grey	SEPTEMBER–FEBRUARY
Carp	ALL YEAR	Mussels	SEPTEMBER–MARCH
Clams	ALL YEAR	Octopus	ALL YEAR
Cockles	MAY–DECEMBER	Perch	ALL YEAR
Cod	JUNE–FEBRUARY	Pike	AUGUST–FEBRUARY
Conger eel	MARCH–OCTOBER	Plaice	MAY–FEBRUARY
Coley	AUGUST–FEBRUARY	Prawns	ALL YEAR
Crab	APRIL–DECEMBER	Salmon	ALL YEAR
Flounder	MARCH–NOVEMBER	Sardines	FEBRUARY–JULY
Haddock	ALL YEAR, BEST MAY–FEBRUARY	Scallops and Queens	SEPTEMBER–MARCH
Hake	JUNE–MARCH	Shrimps	FEBRUARY–OCTOBER
Halibut	ALL YEAR, BEST JUNE–MARCH	Skate	MAY–FEBRUARY
Herring	MAY–DECEMBER	Sole	
Huss (Rockfish, Dogfish)	ALL YEAR	– Lemon	MAY–MARCH
		– Dover	MAY–FEBRUARY
		– Witch or Torbay	BEST AUGUST–APRIL
John Dory	ALL YEAR	Sprats	OCTOBER–MARCH
Langoustine (Dublin Bay prawns, Scampi, Norway lobster)	APRIL–NOVEMBER	Squid	MAY–OCTOBER
		Swordfish	ALL YEAR
Lobster	APRIL–NOVEMBER	Trout	
Mackerel	ALL YEAR	– Rainbow	ALL YEAR
		– Sea (Salmon)	FEBRUARY–AUGUST
Monkfish (Angler fish)	ALL YEAR	Tuna	ALL YEAR
		Turbot	APRIL–FEBRUARY
		Whiting	JUNE–FEBRUARY

BUYING FROZEN FISH AND SHELLFISH

Frozen fish are usually sold as cutlets or fillets. Shellfish are usually sold removed from their shells. Always choose firmly frozen undamaged packets and buy from a reputable fishmonger or supermarket. Buy slightly more shellfish than the recipe calls for to allow for weight-loss after thawing.

White fish will keep in the freezer for about 3 months and oily fish and shellfish for 2 months. After this the flavour and texture deteriorate.

THAWING FISH AND SHELLFISH

Thaw in the microwave following the chart below, or thaw overnight in the coolest part of the refrigerator. Do not thaw in water as flavour, texture and nutrients will be lost.

CLEANING FISH

The fishmonger will nearly always prepare fish for you, but you can do it yourself following these instructions:

1 Using the back of a knife, remove any scales, scraping from tail to head (the opposite way to the direction the scales lie). As the scales may fly everywhere it is a good idea to do this in the sink. Rinse under cold running water.

2 To remove the entrails from round fish, such as herrings or trout, make a slit along the belly from the gills to the tail vent. Draw out the insides and clean away any blood. Rub with a little salt to remove the black skin. Rinse under cold water.

3 To remove the entrails from flat fish, such as sole and plaice, open the cavity which lies in the upper part of the body under the gills and clean out the entrails as above. Rinse under cold water.

4 Cut off the fins and gills, if wished, if the fish is to be served whole. The head and tail may also be cut off. If your cooker has a turntable it may be necessary to remove the head and tail from larger fish to ensure that they fit in the cooker. Rinse the fish under cold running water and dry with absorbent kitchen paper.

SKINNING FISH

Whole flat fish

1 Rinse the fish and cut off the fins, if not already removed. Make an incision across the tail, slip your

THAWING FISH AND SHELLFISH

Separate cutlets, fillets or steaks as soon as possible during thawing, and remove pieces from the cooker as soon as they are thawed. Timing will depend on the thickness of the fish.

TYPE	TIME/SETTING	NOTES
Whole round fish (mullet trout, carp, bream, whiting)	4–6 minutes per 450 g (1 lb) on LOW or DEFROST	Stand for 5 minutes after each 2–3 minutes. Very large fish are thawed more successfully if left to stand for 10–15 minutes after every 2–3 minutes.
White fish fillets or cutlets (cod, coley, haddock, halibut, monkfish), whole plaice or sole	3–4 minutes per 450 g (1 lb) on LOW or DEFROST	Stand for 5 minutes after each 2–3 minutes.
Lobster, crab, crab claws	6–8 minutes per 450 g (1 lb) on LOW or DEFROST	Stand for 5 minutes after each 2–3 minutes.
Crab meat	4–6 minutes per 450 g (1 lb) block on LOW or DEFROST	Stand for 5 minutes after each 2–3 minutes.
Prawns, shrimps, scampi, scallops	2–3 minutes per 100 g (4 oz) 3–4 minutes per 225 g (8 oz) on LOW or DEFROST	Arrange in a circle on a double sheet of absorbent kitchen paper to absorb liquid. Separate during thawing with a fork and remove pieces from cooker as they thaw.

thumb between the skin and the flesh and loosen the dark skin around the sides of the fish.

2   Salt your fingers to make it easier to grip, then hold the fish down firmly with one hand and hold the skin with the other hand. Then pull the skin upwards towards the head. The white skin can be removed in the same way, but unless the fish is particularly large, this layer of skin is usually left on.

Fillet of flat fish

1   Lay the fillet on a board, skin side down. Salt your fingers and hold the tail end of the skin firmly. Insert a sharp knife between the flesh and the skin and work from head to tail, sawing with the knife from side to side and pressing the flat side of the blade against the skin. Keep the edges of the blade close to the skin while cutting, but do not press it down at too sharp an angle or you will slice through the fish's skin.

Round fish

These are usually cooked with the skin on and slashed to prevent splitting during cooking. They may be skinned if wished.

1   Using a sharp knife, cut along the spine and across the skin just below the head. Loosen the skin under the head with the point of the knife. Salt your fingers, then gently pull the skin down towards the tail, working carefully to avoid breaking the flesh. Skin the other side in the same way.

FILLETING FISH

Flat fish

Four fillets are taken from flat fish, two from each side. However, some fishmongers and supermarkets cut only one fillet from each side to make two double or butterfly fillets. These should be cut in half lengthways before beginning any recipes in this book.

1   Using a small, sharp, pointed knife, make an incision straight down the back of the fish, following the line of the bone and keeping the fish flat on the board.

2   Insert the knife between the flesh and the bone and carefully remove the flesh with long, clean strokes, cutting the first fillet from the left-hand side of the fish, carefully working from the head to the tail.

3   Turn the fish and cut off the second fillet from tail to head. Fillet the other side using the same method. There should not be any flesh left on the bone when the fillets are removed.

Round fish

Two fillets are taken from round fish.

1   Keeping the fish flat on the board, cut along the centre of the back close to the backbone, then cut along the belly.

2   Remove the flesh cleanly from the bones, working from the head down, pressing the knife against the bones and working with short, sharp strokes. Remove the fillet from the other side in the same way. If the fish is large, cut the fillets into serving-size pieces.

Herring, mackerel and sardines

These are small fish and are often cooked whole rather than in fillets. This is how to remove the bones:

1   Cut off the head, tail and fins. Split the fish along the belly and remove the entrails. Salt your fingers and rub off the black inner skin and blood.

2   Put the fish on a board, cut side down, and press lightly with your fingers down the middle of the back to loosen the bone.

3   Turn the fish over and ease the backbone up with your fingers, removing with it as many of the small bones as possible. If the fish contains roes, remove these before easing out the backbone (they can be cooked and served with the fish or served separately, if preferred).

PREPARING SQUID

Fishmongers sometimes sell squid ready-prepared. As a rough guide, 350 g (12 oz) prepared squid is equivalent to 450 g (1 lb) unprepared.

1   Rinse the squid, then hold the body in one hand and with the other, firmly pull on the head and tentacles. As you do this, the soft contents of the body will come out and can be discarded. Cut the tentacles just in front of the eyes. Remove the ink sac from the head.

2   Remove the plastic-like quill and rinse the body under cold running water to remove any white substance.

3   Rub the fine dark skin off the outer body and rinse again under cold running water. Cut the flesh into rings or pieces or keep whole for filling with stuffing.

PREPARING OCTOPUS

1   Rinse the octopus, then hold the body in one hand and with the other firmly pull off the head

and tentacles. The soft contents of the body will come out and can be discarded. Cut the tentacles just in front of the eyes.

2   Rinse the body and the tentacles, then beat well with a wooden mallet. Cut the flesh into rings or pieces or keep whole for stuffing. The ink sac has a musky flavour and is not usually used.

PREPARING MUSSELS

Mussels are usually sold in the shell. They are also available ready cooked and frozen in 350 g (1 lb) bags. 450 g (1 lb) shelled mussels is roughly equivalent to 900 g (2 lb) mussels in the shell.

1   Put the mussels into a large bowl and, under running cold water, scrape off any mud, barnacles, seaweed and 'beards' with a small sharp knife. Discard any that are open and do not close when sharply tapped with the back of a knife. Rinse again until there is no trace of sand in the bowl. To cook (see chart on page 14).

PREPARING COCKLES

Cockles are usually sold removed from their shells and cooked – so only need gently reheating. They are sometimes sold by the pint rather than by weight – 1 pint is equal to 350 g (12 oz). They are also available frozen in bags. Prepare cockles in their shells as follows:

1   Rinse well under cold running water, then leave to soak for 2–3 hours before cooking. To cook (see chart on page 14).

PREPARING SCALLOPS

Scallops are available in the shell or removed from the shell, either fresh or frozen. See the chart on page 14 for cooking shelled scallops. Scallops in the shell should be cooked conventionally.

1   Scrub the scallops shells under cold running water to remove as much sand as possible. Discard any that are open and do not close when sharply tapped. Place on a baking sheet with their rounded side uppermost. Cook conventionally at 150°C (300°F) mark 2 for about 10 minutes, or until the shells start to open.

2   Using your fingers, gently push the shells slightly apart until there is a gap into which a knife blade can be slipped. Slide the blade through the opening against the rounded upper shell, then gradually ease the scallop flesh away from the top shell.

3   Detach the scallop from the top shell and prise apart the top and bottom shells by pushing the shell backwards until the small hinge at its base snaps. Rinse the scallops, still attached to the lower shells, under cold running water to remove as much sand as possible.

4   Using a small knife, cut and ease away all the grey-coloured beard-like fringe surrounding the scallop. Make sure that you don't detach the orange roe and try not to tear the flesh.

5   Slide the point of a small knife under the black thread on the side of the scallop. Ease this up and gently pull it off, with the attached black intestinal bag. Ease the scallop away from the bottom shell, wash in a bowl of cold water until all traces of sand have gone. Scrub the rounded shells thoroughly to remove all traces of sand and grit; drain carefully under cold running water and gently pat dry with absorbent kitchen paper.

PREPARING CLAMS

Small clams can be cooked in the microwave (see the chart on page 14), but large clams should be cooked conventionally.

1   Scrub large clams with a stiff scrubbing brush. Hold each clam in a cloth or glove in the palm of one hand and prise open the shells at the hinge (it is helpful if you get a special clam knife for doing this). If the clams are very difficult to open put them into a very hot conventional oven for 5–10 minutes or until they start to open.

2   Loosen the clams, leaving them in one half-shell. Reserve any liquid from the clams and incorporate into a sauce.

PREPARING LOBSTER

It is not humane to cook live lobster in the microwave. Buy ready cooked from your fishmonger or follow one of the methods below.

1   Boil a large saucepan of water vigorously, then let it become completely cold. Immerse the lobster in the water and leave for 30 minutes. The lack of oxygen renders the lobster unconscious before it is put over the heat. Bring to the boil slowly, then simmer gently for 8 minutes per 450 g (1 lb). Lift the lobster out of the pan, set it aside and leave to cool completely.

2   Alternatively, bring a large saucepan of water to the boil, grasp the lobster by the back and drop it into the water, covering the pan with a lid and weight it down for the first 2 minutes. Then simmer gently for 12 minutes for the first 450 g (1 lb), 10 minutes for the next 450 g (1 lb) and 5 minutes more for each additional 450 g (1 lb). Lift out of the pan, set aside and leave to cool completely.

3   If preferred you can kill a lobster before cooking it so it is not overcooked. Keeping your hands clear of the claws, put the lobster, shell side up on a work surface. Place a cleaver in the centre of the cross-shaped mark behind the head and hammer it down with one sharp blow. The lobster may still twitch a little, but that is only a reflex action. Cook the lobster in the same way as for method 2.

4   To remove the meat from the cooked lobster, place it on a firm surface and twist off the claws and pincers. Crack open the large claws and remove the flesh, discarding the membrane from the claw centre. Reserve the smaller claws, which are used only for garnishing.

5   Using a sharp pointed knife, split the lobster in two from head to tail. Remove and discard the intestine (which looks like a small vein running through the centre of the tail), the stomach (which lies near the head), and the spongy-looking gills, which are not edible. Take out the tail flesh, reserving the coral if there is any. Scrape the meat from the rear legs with a skewer.

PREPARING CRAB

Live crabs should be cooked conventionally. Crab meat is also sold frozen in 450 g (1 lb) packets.

1   Place the crab in a large saucepan in enough cold, well salted water to cover. Bring to the boil and boil fairly rapidly for 10 minutes. Leave to cool in the water.

2   Place the crab on its back on a large chopping board. Take a claw firmly in one hand, holding it as close to the body of the crab as possible. Twist it off, steadying the body with the other hand. Remove the other claw and the legs in the same way. Snap the claws in half by bending them backwards at the joint.

3   Hold the claws at the top end and, with a hammer or heavy weight, tap the shell smartly on the rounded edge to crack the claws open. Try not to shatter the shell. Repeat with second claw. Using a blunt knife, ease the white meat out of the claws. Keep the blade as close to the edges of the shell as possible. Using a teaspoon handle or skewer, reach well into the crevices to make sure all the white meat is removed. Discard any membrane.

4   Crack the larger legs open and scrape out the white meat. Keep the small legs for decoration. Reserve all the scooped-out white meat in one bowl.

5   Place the crab on its back with the tail flap towards you, head away from you. Hold the shell firmly and press the body section upwards from beneath the tail flap and ease out with your thumbs until the body is detached. Pull off the inedible, grey feather-like gills (known as dead men's fingers) from the body section and discard them. Use a spoon to remove the stomach bag and mouth which are attached to the back shell. If the bag breaks, make sure you remove all the greenish or grey-white matter.

6   Ease the brown meat out of the shell, running a knife around the edge to bring it out smoothly. Put into a separate bowl. Discard any membrane and scrape out corners of the shell with the handle of a teaspoon.

7   Protecting your hand with a cloth, hold the shell firmly and tap with a hammer just inside natural line of shell until the inner shell breaks smoothly away. Scrub the shell well under cold running water. Then dry the empty shell on absorbent kitchen paper and rub the outside lightly with oil. Place the body on its back on the board. Cut through the body to divide it in two. Spoon any creamy brown meat out into the bowl with the rest. Discard the body pieces.

PREPARING PRAWNS

1   To peel prawns, hold the head of the prawn between the thumb and forefinger of the right hand. Using the fingers of the left hand, hold the tail and gently pinch and pull off the tail shell. Holding the body, gently pull off the head, the body shell and the claws.

2   Using a skewer or the point of a knife, carefully remove and discard the black vein running down the prawn's back.

COOKING FISH IN THE MICROWAVE

Fish is best cooked in a single layer in a large shallow dish. Cutlets, or fish pieces, should be arranged with the thinnest parts towards the centre of the dish. The skin of large, whole fish should be slashed in two or three places to prevent it from splitting during cooking, and if cooking more than two whole fish they should be re-arranged halfway through the cooking time. Cover fish during cooking to retain the moisture unless a recipe says otherwise, for example, fish in bread-crumbs should be cooked uncovered so that the coating does not become soggy. Boil-in-the bag fish should have the bag pierced before cooking to let steam escape. Do not attempt to deep fry fish in the microwave.

Fish is cooked when it looks opaque and flakes easily when tested with a fork. Do not overcook or the fish will be dry and tough. Always test before the end of the given cooking time to prevent this happening.

All recipes in this book were tested using the stated weight of fish, for example four 100 g (4 oz) cod steaks. Because of variations in fish sizes and seasons it may not always be possible to buy fish of a corresponding weight. Buy fish of a similar weight and either increase or decrease the cooking time as appropriate (see chart).

FISH AND SHELLFISH COOKING CHART

The cooking time depends on the thickness of the fish as well as the amount being cooked and whether it is cooked whole, in fillets or cut up into smaller pieces. This chart is a guide only. Always check before the end of the calculated cooking time to prevent overcooking. Simply put the fish in a single layer in a shallow dish with 30 ml (2 tbsp) stock, wine, milk or water per 450 g (1 lb) of fish (unless otherwise stated), then cover and cook as below.

TYPE	TIME/SETTING	NOTES
Whole round fish (whiting, mullet, trout, carp, bream, small haddock)	4 minutes on HIGH per 450 g (1 lb)	Slash skin to prevent bursting. Turn fish over halfway through cooking time if fish weighs more than 1.4 kg (3 lb). Re-position fish if cooking more than two.
Whole flat fish (plaice, sole)	3 minutes on HIGH per 450 g (1 lb)	Slash skin. Check fish after 2 minutes.
Cutlets, steaks, thick fish fillets (cod, coley, haddock, halibut, monkfish fillet)	4 minutes on HIGH per 450 g (1 lb)	Position thicker parts towards the outside of the dish. Turn halfway through cooking if steaks are very thick.
Flat fish fillets (plaice, sole)	2–3 minutes on HIGH per 450 g (1 lb)	Check fish after 2 minutes.
Dense fish fillets, cutlets, steaks (tuna, swordfish, conger eel), whole monkfish tail	5–6 minutes on HIGH per 450 g (1 lb)	Position thicker parts towards the outside of the dish. Turn halfway through cooking if steaks are thick.
Skate wings	6–7 minutes on HIGH per 450 g (1 lb)	Add 150 ml (¼ pint) stock or milk. If cooking more than 900 g (2 lb) cook in batches.
Smoked fish	Cook as appropriate for type of fish, e.g. whole, fillet or cutlet. See above	
Squid	Put prepared squid, cut into rings in a large bowl with 150 ml (¼ pint) wine, stock or water per 450 g (1 lb) of squid. Cook, covered, on HIGH for 5–8 minutes per 450 g (1 lb)	Time depends on size of squid – larger, older, squid are tougher and may take longer to cook.
Octopus	Put prepared octopus, cut into 2.5 cm (1 inch) pieces in a large bowl with 150 ml (¼ pint) wine, stock or water per 450 g (1 lb) of octopus. Cook, covered, on HIGH until liquid is boiling, then on MEDIUM for 15–20 minutes per 450 g (1 lb)	Tenderise octopus before cooking by beating vigorously with a meat mallet or rolling pin. Marinate before cooking to help tenderise. Time depends on age and size of octopus.

Scallops (shelled)	2–4 minutes on HIGH per 450 g (1 lb)	Do not overcook or scallops will be tough. Add corals for 1–2 minutes at end of cooking time.
Scallops in their shells	Do not cook in the microwave	Cook conventionally (see page 12).
Mussels	Put up to 900 g (2 lb) mussels in a large bowl with 150 ml (¼ pint) wine, stock or water. Cook, covered, on HIGH for 3–5 minutes	Remove mussels on the top as they cook. Shake the bowl occasionally during cooking. Discard any mussels which do not open.
Cockles	Put cockles in a large bowl with a little water. Cook, covered, on HIGH for 3–4 minutes until the shells open. Take cockles out of their shells and cook for a further 2–3 minutes or until hot	Shake the bowl occasionally during cooking.
Oysters	Do not cook in the microwave	
Raw prawns	2–5 minutes on HIGH per 450 g (1 lb), stirring frequently	Time depends on the size of the prawns. Cook until their colour changes to bright pink.
Live lobster	Do not cook in the microwave	Cook conventionally (see page 12).
Live crab	Do not cook in the microwave	Cook conventionally (see page 13).
Small clams	Cook as mussels	As mussels.
Large clams	Do not cook in the microwave	Cook conventionally (see page 12).

· BREAKFAST AND BRUNCH ·

Breakfast as a proper meal is a rapidly disappearing British tradition. Busy lifestyles mean that breakfast is missed or completely reduced to a slice of toast or a bowl of muesli. But with the help of a microwave oven, it is possible to produce a delicious hot breakfast in just a few minutes. Nutritionists agree that we should start the day with breakfast, and what could be healthier than a breakfast based on fish? This chapter includes a selection of favourite breakfast dishes such as Kedgeree as well as substantial brunch recipes for late, lazy weekends.

· *MACKEREL WITH ORANGE AND MUSTARD* ·

A fresh orange salad contrasts well with mackerel in this attractive summer breakfast dish.

SERVES 2–4

2 small oranges
15 ml (1 tbsp) mild wholegrain
 mustard

salt and pepper
4 fresh mackerel fillets, each weighing
 about 100 g (4 oz)

·

1 FINELY grate the rind from one of the oranges. Mix with the mustard and the juice of half an orange to make a soft paste. Season to taste.

·

2 BRUSH the mackerel on both sides with the paste and arrange in a single layer in a shallow dish. Cover and cook on HIGH for 4–5 minutes or until the fish flakes easily.

·

3 MEANWHILE, remove all the skin and pith from the remaining half and whole oranges, cut into very thin slices and arrange on two or four plates. Arrange the mackerel on the plates with the orange slices and serve immediately, with warm bread.

Warm Croissant with Smoked Mackerel and Watercress Butter (page 17)

WARM CROISSANT WITH SMOKED MACKEREL AND WATERCRESS BUTTER ▪

These deliciously rich croissants are just as good if made in advance and stored overnight in the refrigerator. If cooking them straight from the refrigerator, increase the cooking time in step 5 to 2–3 minutes.

SERVES 4

50 g (2 oz) butter
finely grated rind and juice of ½ a
    lemon
½ a small bunch of watercress

2 smoked mackerel fillets
salt and pepper
cayenne pepper (optional)
4 croissants

▪

1 PUT the butter into a medium bowl and cook on LOW for 1–2 minutes until slightly softened. Beat until smooth, then gradually beat in the lemon rind and juice.

▪

2 FINELY chop half the watercress, discarding any tough stems, and beat into the butter.

▪

3 FLAKE the fish and mix carefully into the butter being careful not to mash the flakes of fish. Season to taste with salt, pepper and cayenne pepper.

▪

4 CUT each croissant in half horizontally and spread the fish butter on one side of each. Lay the remaining sprigs of watercress on top of the butter.

▪

5 SANDWICH the croissants together again, wrap each one loosely in a napkin and cook on HIGH for 1–2 minutes until warm. (*Note*: one croissant will take 30 seconds.) Serve immediately, wrapped in the napkin.

Japanese Clear Soup with Prawns (page 36) and Waterzooi (page 32)

▪ DEVILLED HERRINGS IN OATMEAL ▪

Herrings in oatmeal are a traditional breakfast or supper dish in Scotland.
Here they are devilled to give them extra flavour.

SERVES 2

10 ml (2 level tsp) tomato purée
2.5 ml (½ level tsp) mild mustard
2.5 ml (½ level tsp) brown sugar
dash of Worcestershire sauce
pinch of cayenne pepper
salt and pepper

4 small herring fillets
60 ml (4 level tbsp) medium oatmeal
15 ml (1 tbsp) vegetable oil
15 g (½ oz) butter or margarine
lemon wedges, to garnish

▪

1 HEAT a browning dish on HIGH for 5–8 minutes or according to the manufacturer's instructions.

▪

2 MEANWHILE, mix the tomato purée, mustard, sugar, Worcestershire sauce and cayenne pepper together. Season to taste with salt and pepper. Spread the paste thinly on to both sides of each fillet, then coat in the oatmeal.

▪

3 PUT the oil and butter or margarine into the browning dish and swirl it around to coat the base of the dish.

▪

4 QUICKLY add the fillets, skin side down, and cook on HIGH for 1½ minutes. Turn over and cook on HIGH for 1–2 minutes or until tender. Serve the herrings immediately, garnished with lemon wedges.

▪ COCOTTE EGGS WITH SMOKED FISH ▪

A cocotte is a French word meaning a small earthenware or porcelain dish
used for baking egg dishes. If you do not have authentic cocotte dishes, use
any small heatproof dishes which are suitable for cooking
and serving in.

SERVES 4

225 g (8 oz) smoked fish fillets, such as
   haddock, mackerel or trout
black pepper
4 eggs

60 ml (4 tbsp) double cream or Greek
   strained yogurt
mushroom ketchup

▪

1 SKIN the fish, cut into small pieces and divide between four 150 ml (¼ pint) dishes. Season with black pepper.

2 CRACK an egg into each dish and carefully prick each yolk twice, using a cocktail stick.

■

3 FLAVOUR the cream or yogurt with mushroom ketchup and black pepper, then carefully spoon the mixture on top of the eggs.

■

4 ARRANGE the dishes in a circle in the cooker. Cook on MEDIUM for 5–6 minutes until the eggs look almost set, turning once if the eggs are cooking unevenly. Leave to stand for 1 minute, then serve with toasted bread or muffins.

■ *SMOKED TROUT CUSTARDS* ■

Make sure that you cook these custards on MEDIUM; if overcooked they will curdle.

SERVES 4

1 smoked trout, weighing about 225 g (8 oz)
100 g (4 oz) cream cheese
45 ml (3 tbsp) natural yogurt
15 ml (1 tbsp) horseradish sauce

5 ml (1 level tsp) cornflour
1 egg, separated
salt and pepper
ground cloves (optional)

■

1 REMOVE and discard the trout skin and bones. Flake the flesh and mix with the cheese, yogurt, horseradish sauce, cornflour and egg yolk.

■

2 WHISK the egg white until stiff and fold in. Season with salt and pepper.

■

3 SPOON the mixture into four 150 ml (¼ pint) ramekin dishes and sprinkle a pinch of ground cloves over the top of each.

■

4 ARRANGE the dishes in a circle in the cooker and cook on MEDIUM for 5–6 minutes until lightly set around the edge but still soft in the centre. Leave to stand for 2–3 minutes, then serve with brown bread and butter.

▪ *FISHCAKES* ▪

Homemade fishcakes are far superior to the bought kind. This recipe uses freshly cooked fish, but is equally good made with ready cooked smoked fish such as trout or mackerel or canned fish such as tuna or salmon.

MAKES 4

2 medium potatoes, each weighing
   about 100 g (4 oz)
225 g (8 oz) fish fillets, such as smoked
   haddock, cod, salmon or coley
30 ml (2 tbsp) milk
25 g (1 oz) butter or margarine
finely grated rind of ½ a lemon

30 ml (2 tbsp) chopped fresh parsley
few drops anchovy essence
salt and pepper
beaten egg
30 ml (2 tbsp) seasoned plain flour
30 ml (2 tbsp) vegetable oil

▪

1 SCRUB the potatoes and prick all over with a fork. Cook on HIGH for 7 minutes. Turn the potatoes over.

▪

2 PUT the fish and the milk into a small shallow dish. Cover and put into the cooker with the potatoes. Cook on HIGH for 4–5 minutes until the fish flakes easily and the potatoes are soft.

▪

3 FLAKE the fish, discarding the skin, and put into a bowl with the cooking liquid. Cut the potatoes in half, scoop out the flesh and add to the fish.

▪

4 HEAT a browning dish on HIGH for 5–8 minutes or according to manufacturer's instructions.

▪

5 MEANWHILE, mix the fish and potato with the butter or margarine, lemon rind, half the parsley, the anchovy essence and salt and pepper to taste. Mash thoroughly together, then mix with enough beaten egg to bind.

▪

6 SHAPE into four fishcakes about 2.5 cm (1 inch) thick. Mix the remaining parsley with the seasoned flour and use to coat the fishcakes.

▪

7 ADD the oil to the browning dish, then quickly add the fishcakes and cook on HIGH for 2½ minutes. Turn over and cook on HIGH for a further 2 minutes. Serve immediately.

▪ *SCRAMBLED EGGS WITH SMOKED SALMON* ▪

Smoked salmon is delicious with scrambled eggs, cooked to perfection in the microwave and it need not be expensive if you use smoked salmon trimmings.

SERVES 2

4 eggs
60 ml (4 tbsp) milk or cream
25 g (1 oz) butter or margarine
  (optional)

50 g (2 oz) smoked salmon trimmings
salt and pepper

▪

1 PUT the eggs, milk or cream and butter or margarine into a medium bowl and whisk together with a balloon whisk.

▪

2 COOK on HIGH for 2 minutes or until the mixture just begins to set around the edge. Whisk vigorously to incorporate the set egg mixture, then cook on HIGH for a further 1–2 minutes or until the eggs are just set, whisking every minute.

▪

3 USING kitchen scissors snip the salmon trimmings into the egg mixture and mix gently together. Season to taste with salt and pepper, then serve immediately with hot buttered toast.

▪ *LOX AND BAGELS* ▪

Everybodies favourite brunch dish – follow the basic method and alter the filling to suit your taste if preferred.

SERVES 1

1 bagel
25 g (1 oz) cream cheese

1 slice of smoked salmon

▪

1 WRAP the bagel in a paper napkin or a piece of absorbent kitchen paper and cook on HIGH for 30 seconds until just warm.

▪

2 SPLIT in half and fill with the cream cheese and salmon. Serve wrapped in the napkin. Eat immediately!

▪

Note:
2 bagels, cook on HIGH for 45–60 seconds
3 bagels, cook on HIGH for 1–1½ minutes
4 bagels, cook on HIGH for 1½–2 minutes
Do not heat more than four bagels at once.

· KEDGEREE ·

Kedgeree was originally an Indian dish called khicharhi which contained lentils and spices.

SERVES 4–6

175 g (6 oz) basmati or long grain
    white rice
75 g (3 oz) green lentils
450 g (1 lb) smoked haddock fillets
45 ml (3 tbsp) milk
1 large onion, skinned and chopped
10 ml (2 level tsp) coriander seeds

2 cloves
2 cardamoms
15 ml (1 tbsp) vegetable oil
finely grated rind and juice of 1 lime
25 g (1 oz) butter or margarine
2 eggs, beaten
chopped fresh coriander or parsley

1 PUT the rice and lentils into a large bowl and pour over enough boiling water to cover by about 2.5 cm (1 inch). Leave to soak while cooking the fish.

2 PUT the haddock into the middle of a large serving dish with a flat bottom and pour over the milk. Sprinkle the onion around the edge of the dish. Cover and cook on HIGH for 4–5 minutes or until the fish flakes easily. Remove the fish.

3 CRUSH the coriander seeds, cloves and cardamoms and put into the serving dish with the oil. Stir together to coat the spices and onion in oil.

4 PUT the bowl containing the rice, lentils and water into the cooker and stand the dish containing the onion and spices on top of it.

5 COOK on HIGH for 10–12 minutes or until the water is boiling, stirring the onion and spices once. When the water is boiling, remove the dish containing the onion and spices and set aside.

6 CONTINUE to cook the rice and lentils, uncovered, on HIGH for 10 minutes or until tender, and all of the water is absorbed, stirring occasionally.

7 MEANWHILE, flake the fish and mix into the onion and spices with the lime rind and juice and the butter or margarine.

8 WHEN the lentils and rice are cooked, carefully mix with the fish.

9 COOK on HIGH for 2 minutes or until hot. Lightly mix in the eggs using a fork (the heat of the mixture will cook the eggs). Season to taste with salt and pepper, and sprinkle generously with chopped coriander or parsley. Serve immediately.

▪ POACHED KIPPER WITH TOMATO ▪

Kipper with tomato makes a very quick and nutritious breakfast; try to buy naturally smoked kipper fillet rather than the kind containing artificial colour.

SERVES 1

1 kipper fillet, weighing about 175 g
  (6 oz)
lemon juice

pinch of ground mace
black pepper
1 large tomato

▪

1 PLACE the kipper fillet towards the edge of a plate. Sprinkle with lemon juice and season to taste with mace and black pepper.

▪

2 CUT the tomato in half and place on the plate with the kipper.

▪

3 COVER loosely with absorbent kitchen paper and cook on HIGH for 2–3 minutes or until hot. Serve immediately, with hot buttered toast or Fried anchovy bread (page 24)

▪ SARDINES WITH LEMON AND PARSLEY ▪

Sardines, although oily fish, contain polyunsaturated fats, and are a very healthy food.

SERVES 4

8 fresh or thawed frozen sardines,
  cleaned
15 ml (1 tbsp) olive oil
grated rind and juice of 1 lemon

60 ml (4 tbsp) chopped fresh parsley
salt and pepper
lemon wedges, to garnish

▪

1 WASH the sardines and scrape off the scales. Using a sharp knife, make two diagonal slashes on each side of each fish.

▪

2 PUT the oil into a shallow dish large enough to hold the fish in a single layer and cook on HIGH for 30 seconds until hot. Arrange the fish in the dish and cook on HIGH for 3 minutes.

▪

3 TURN the fish over and sprinkle with the lemon rind and juice, parsley and salt and pepper to taste. Cook on HIGH for a further 2–3 minutes or until the fish is tender. Serve garnished with lemon wedges.

· COD AND TARRAGON STUFFED BAGUETTE ·

Use a small baguette, or half a large French loaf. This recipe can be made in advance up to step 3 and then cooked in the morning, increasing the cooking time by 1–2 minutes.

SERVES 4

450 g (1 lb) cod or haddock fillets
30 ml (2 tbsp) milk
100 g (4 oz) cream cheese with garlic
   and herbs
25 g (1 oz) butter or margarine

10 ml (2 tsp) chopped fresh tarragon
lemon juice
salt and pepper
1 small baguette

1 PUT the cod into a large shallow dish and pour over the milk. Cover and cook on HIGH for 4–5 minutes or until the fish flakes easily.

2 FLAKE the fish and put into a bowl with the cream cheese, butter or margarine and tarragon. Beat together until well mixed, then add the lemon juice and salt and pepper to taste.

3 CUT the baguette into four even-sized pieces. Using a long sharp knife, cut out the centre of each piece of bread. Tear into small pieces and beat into the fish mixture to make a stuffing. Use the stuffing to fill the bread shells.

4 WRAP each piece in a napkin and cook on HIGH for 2–3 minutes or until just heated through. Serve immediately wrapped in the napkin.

· FRIED ANCHOVY BREAD ·

Anchovy purée is a paste of anchovies, salt and oil which is sold in tubes in delicatessens and supermarkets. Fried Anchovy Bread is the perfect accompaniment to Poached Kipper with Tomato (see page 23).

SERVES 2

4 large slices of day-old bread
20 ml (4 tsp) anchovy purée
1 egg

75 ml (3 fl oz) milk
black pepper
30 ml (2 tbsp) vegetable oil

1 HEAT a browning dish on HIGH for 5–8 minutes or according to the manufacturer's instructions.

2 CUT the crusts off the bread and cut each slice in half. Spread both sides of the bread with the anchovy purée.

3 PUT the egg, milk, and black pepper into a shallow dish and beat together until well mixed. Dip the bread in the milk mixture, making sure each piece is completely covered.

■

4 ADD the oil to the browning dish, swirling it around to coat the base completely. Quickly add the bread in a single layer and cook on HIGH for 1 minute, then turn over and cook on HIGH for 1–2 minutes until crisp. Serve immediately.

■ *POTTED SHRIMPS* ■

Shrimps are very small crustaceans similar to small prawns. They are greyish brown in colour when alive and pink when cooked. They are not always available fresh, but can be bought frozen.

SERVES 4

200 g (7 oz) butter
175 g (6 oz) cooked shrimps, peeled
pinch of ground mace

pinch of cayenne pepper
pinch of ground nutmeg
salt and pepper

■

1 CUT half the butter into small pieces, put into a medium bowl and cook on HIGH for 1–2 minutes until melted.

■

2 ADD the shrimps, mace, cayenne pepper, nutmeg, salt and plenty of pepper. Stir to coat the shrimps in the butter, then cook on LOW for 2–3 minutes until the shrimps are hot. Do not allow the mixture to boil. Pour into four ramekin dishes or small pots.

■

3 CUT the remaining butter into small pieces, put into a medium bowl and cook on HIGH for 1–2 minutes until melted. Leave to stand for a few minutes while the salt and sediment settle, then carefully spoon the clarified butter over the shrimps to cover completely. Leave until set, then chill in the refrigerator before serving.

■

4 SERVE straight from the pots with brown bread and lemon wedges, or turn out and arrange on individual plates.

▪ *FISH PILAFF* ▪

This is definitely a brunch dish as it's quite substantial; it can be made in advance and reheated successfully – simply sprinkle with about 30 ml (2 tbsp) water, cover and cook on HIGH for 3–5 minutes or until hot.

SERVES 6

25 g (1 oz) flaked almonds
15 ml (1 tbsp) vegetable oil
1 onion, skinned and chopped
1 garlic clove, skinned and crushed
10 ml (2 level tsp) ground cinnamon
5 ml (1 level tsp) ground turmeric
350 g (12 oz) long grain rice
450 g (1 lb) white fish fillets, such as haddock, cod, coley or whiting, skinned

105 g (4 oz) can smoked mussels in olive oil
50 g (2 oz) sultanas
salt and pepper
45 ml (3 tbsp) chopped fresh parsley

▪

1 SPREAD the almonds out on a plate and cook on HIGH for 4–6 minutes or until lightly browned, stirring once. Set aside.

▪

2 PUT the oil, onion, garlic, cinnamon and turmeric into a large dish. Cover and cook on HIGH for 3–4 minutes or until the onion is slightly softened.

▪

3 ADD the rice and stir to coat in the oil. Pour over 600 ml (1 pint) boiling water, re-cover and cook on HIGH for 14–15 minutes or until the rice is tender. Meanwhile, cut the fish into 5 cm (2 inch) cubes.

▪

4 ARRANGE the fish in a single layer on top of the rice and pour over 30 ml (2 tbsp) water. Cover and cook on HIGH for 3–4 minutes or until the fish is just cooked.

▪

5 LIGHTLY stir the fish into the rice being careful not to break up the pieces. Add the mussels with the oil from the can and the sultanas and season to taste with salt and pepper.

▪

6 COVER and cook on HIGH for 2–3 minutes or until hot. Sprinkle with the almonds and the parsley and serve immediately.

· SOUPS ·

There is nothing to beat the flavour of good homemade
soup. Once you have tried making soup for yourself you
will find that it is surprisingly easy and very quick in the
microwave cooker. Homemade fish stock gives the best
flavour (see page 125) but vegetable stock, either
homemade or made with a stock cube, can be substituted.
The timings will be shorter if you use a hot stock as
bringing liquid to boiling point in the microwave is a
time-consuming process.

Many of the soups in this chapter are puréed in a blender
or food processor to give a thick, smooth, creamy texture.
If you do not own a food processor, you can use a mouli-
legume or simply mash the mixture with a potato masher
before straining it through a sieve.

· SMOKED HADDOCK CHOWDER ·

*A chowder is an American soup usually made with fish, potatoes and milk.
Using smoked fish gives it extra flavour.*

SERVES 4

1 large onion, skinned
225 g (8 oz) potato, peeled
225 g (8 oz) carrots, scrubbed
2 celery sticks, finely chopped
450 g (1 lb) smoked haddock fillets,
  skinned

568 ml (1 pint) milk
salt and pepper
15 ml (1 tbsp) lemon juice

·

1 GRATE the onion, potato and carrots into a large bowl. Add the celery
and 150 ml (¼ pint) water, cover and cook on HIGH for 12–14 minutes
until the vegetables are softened.

·

2 MEANWHILE, cut the fish into 2.5 cm (1 inch) cubes.

·

3 STIR the fish into the softened vegetables with the milk, salt and
pepper to taste and the lemon juice. Cook on HIGH for 5–6 minutes until
the fish is cooked. Serve immediately.

· CREAM OF FISH AND ROOT VEGETABLE SOUP ·

This nourishing family soup can be made in advance up to the puréeing in step 4. Add the stock and seasoning and store in the refrigerator until required. Reheat on HIGH for 4–5 minutes or until hot, then follow step 5.

SERVES 6

100 g (4 oz) carrots, peeled
100 g (4 oz) parsnips, peeled
100 g (4 oz) swede, peeled
1 medium onion, skinned
25 g (1 oz) butter or margarine
1 litre (1¾ pints) fish or vegetable stock
  (see pages 125 and 123)

450 g (1 lb) white fish fillets, such as
  cod, coley or haddock, skinned
salt and pepper
150 ml (¼ pint) single cream
chopped fresh parsley, to garnish

·

1 GRATE the vegetables and put into a large bowl with the butter or margarine and half the fish or vegetable stock. Cover and cook on HIGH for 10–15 minutes or until the vegetables are very soft.

·

2 MEANWHILE, cut the fish into small pieces.

·

3 ADD the fish to the softened vegetables and cook on HIGH for 3–4 minutes or until the fish flakes easily.

·

4 PURÉE the soup in a blender or food processor and return to the rinsed-out bowl. Add the remaining stock and season to taste with salt and pepper. Cook on HIGH for 3–4 minutes or until hot.

·

5 STIR in the cream and cook on HIGH for 1 minute, but do not allow the soup to boil or it will curdle. Serve hot, garnished with chopped parsley.

▪ *INDONESIAN SOUP* ▪

This soup is based on an Indonesian recipe, and uses creamed coconut, peanut butter and tamarind water to give an authentic flavour. Tamarind water is made from tamarind pods which are sold pressed into small blocks, available from ethnic grocers. If you cannot find tamarind, substitute lemon juice but the flavour will not be the same.

SERVES 4–6

25 g (1 oz) tamarind
2 garlic cloves, skinned and crushed
5 cm (2 inch) piece root ginger, peeled
   and finely grated
1 green chilli, seeded and chopped
5 ml (1 level tsp) ground coriander
15 ml (1 tbsp) vegetable oil
75 g (3 oz) creamed coconut
30 ml (2 tbsp) crunchy peanut butter

1 small squid, cleaned (see page 11)
75 g (3 oz) medium egg noodles
175 g (6 oz) peeled scampi or prawns
75 g (3 oz) firm tofu
5 ml (1 tsp) chopped fresh lemon grass
   or lemon rind
salt and pepper
chopped spring onions, to garnish

▪

1 PUT the tamarind and 150 ml (¼ pint) water into a small bowl and leave to soak.

▪

2 MEANWHILE, put the garlic, ginger, chilli, coriander and oil into a large bowl and cook on HIGH for 2 minutes, stirring once.

▪

3 PUT the coconut and peanut butter into a large jug and pour over 900 ml (1½ pints) boiling water. Stir until dissolved, then stir into the spice mixture. Cut the squid into small rings and stir into the soup.

▪

4 COVER and cook on HIGH for 5–6 minutes or until boiling. When the soup is boiling, add the noodles and the scampi or prawns. Re-cover and cook on HIGH for 3–4 minutes or until the soup just returns to the boil and the noodles are tender, stirring occasionally.

▪

5 STRAIN the tamarind and water mixture pressing on the soft pulp to extract the juices. Discard the pulp, then add the brown liquid to the soup.

▪

6 CUT the tofu into 2.5 cm (1 inch) cubes and stir into the soup with the lemon grass or lemon rind and salt and pepper to taste. Reheat on HIGH for 1 minute. Garnish with spring onions, then serve immediately with prawn crackers.

· CREAMY FENNEL AND FLOUNDER SOUP ·

This delicately flavoured soup makes a delicious starter. Because it is very pale in colour it needs garnishing, so if your fennel does not have any feathery fronds, use chopped parsley instead.

SERVES 6

15 ml (1 level tbsp) plain flour
15 ml (1 tbsp) vegetable oil
900 ml (1½ pints) fish or vegetable stock (see pages 125 and 123)
1 small bulb fennel, finely chopped
1 small onion, skinned and finely chopped

450 g (1 lb) flounder, plaice or sole fillets, skinned
150 ml (¼ pint) soured cream
salt and pepper
fennel fronds, to garnish

1 PUT the flour and oil into a large bowl and cook on HIGH for 30 seconds, stirring once.

2 GRADUALLY stir in the stock, fennel and onion. Cook on HIGH for 12–14 minutes until boiling and slightly thickened and the vegetables are tender, stirring occasionally.

3 CUT the fish into small pieces and stir into the soup. Cook on HIGH for 3–4 minutes until the fish is tender, stirring occasionally. Leave to cool slightly, then pour the soup into a blender or food processor and purée until smooth.

4 RETURN the soup to the rinsed-out bowl, stir in the soured cream and season to taste with salt and pepper. Cook on LOW for 2 minutes or until just warmed through, do not allow to boil or the soup will curdle. Serve immediately, garnished with fennel.

· COCKLE AND TOMATO SOUP ·

This is a good way of trying cockles if you have never tasted them before.

SERVES 4

3 anchovy fillets
2 garlic cloves, skinned and crushed
30 ml (2 tbsp) olive oil
900 ml (1½ pints) fish or vegetable stock (see pages 125 and 123)
450 g (1 lb) tomatoes, skinned and sliced

30 ml (2 tbsp) capers
45 ml (3 tbsp) chopped fresh parsley
salt and pepper
300 ml (½ pint) cooked shelled cockles (see chart on page 14)
4 slices of toast

1 Put the anchovies, garlic, and oil into a large bowl and pound together to make a paste.

■

2 Gradually stir in the stock, tomatoes, capers, parsley and salt and pepper to taste. Cover and cook on HIGH for 10 minutes or until boiling, stirring occasionally and taking care not to break up the tomatoes.

■

3 Add the cockles to the soup and cook on HIGH for 2–3 minutes to heat through.

■

4 Place the toast in four soup bowls and carefully ladle the soup on top. Serve immediately.

▪ *SOUPE DE POISSONS* ▪

Use a good mixture of fish and shellfish such as red mullet, red snapper, monkfish, brill, sea bass, conger eel, mussels and prawns for this soup.

Serves 4

30 ml (2 tbsp) olive oil
2 medium onions, skinned and finely chopped
3 garlic cloves, skinned and crushed
226 g (8 oz) can tomatoes, roughly chopped
900 g (2 lb) mixed fish and shellfish
1 bouquet garni

1 strip orange rind
few saffron threads
600 ml (1 pint) fish or vegetable stock (see pages 125 and 123)
salt and pepper
slices of French bread, grated gruyère cheese or Rouille (see page 121), to serve

■

1 Put the oil, onions, garlic and tomatoes into a large bowl. Cover and cook on HIGH for 5–6 minutes until softened.

■

2 Meanwhile, wash the fish and cut into large chunks. Add the fish, including the shells and bones, bouquet garni, orange rind, saffron and half the stock to the tomato mixture. Re-cover and cook on HIGH for 8–10 minutes until all the fish is tender.

■

3 Strain through a sieve, pressing down on the bones and shells of the fish to extract as much liquid and fish as possible.

■

4 Pour the strained liquid into the rinsed-out bowl or a soup tureen and add the remaining stock. Season with salt and pepper then cook on HIGH for 3–4 minutes until hot.

■

5 Serve the soup hot, with the bread sprinkled with cheese or spread with rouille.

· WATERZOOI ·

Waterzooi is a dish originating in Belgium. It is traditionally made with chicken or freshwater fish as here.

SERVES 6

15 ml (1 tbsp) vegetable oil
2.5 ml (½ level tsp) ground cloves
2 celery sticks, chopped
2 leeks, sliced
2 large carrots, scrubbed and thinly sliced
1 bouquet garni
2 strips of lemon rind
600 ml (1 pint) fish or vegetable stock (see pages 125 and 123)

700 g (1½ lb) freshwater fish fillets, such as bream, carp, pike or eel, skinned
salt and pepper
2 egg yolks
150 ml (¼ pint) milk
6 slices of toast
30 ml (2 tbsp) chopped fresh parsley

■

1 PUT the oil, cloves, celery, leeks, carrots, bouquet garni, lemon rind and half the stock into a large bowl. Cover and cook on HIGH for 12–14 minutes or until the vegetables are softened.

■

2 MEANWHILE, cut the fish into bite-sized pieces.

■

3 ADD the fish, remaining stock and salt and pepper to taste to the soup. Re-cover and cook on HIGH for 6–7 minutes or until the fish is cooked.

■

4 MEANWHILE, blend the egg yolks and milk together. When the fish is cooked, spoon a little of the hot liquid on to the egg yolk mixture and mix together. Pour back into the soup.

■

5 RE-COVER and cook on MEDIUM for 1–2 minutes or until thickened, stirring once; do not allow the soup to boil or it will curdle. Discard the lemon rind and bouquet garni.

■

6 To serve, place the toast in six soup bowls, carefully spoon over the soup and garnish with chopped parsley. Serve immediately.

Stuffed Mussels with Pine Nuts and Raisins (page 44)

SCALLOP AND WATERCRESS SOUP ▪

In this soup the scallops make a garnish as well as adding flavour.

SERVES 6

75 g (3 oz) butter or margarine
1 medium onion, skinned and finely
  chopped
2 bunches of watercress
50 g (2 oz) plain flour

900 ml (1½ pints) fish or vegetable
  stock (see pages 125 and 123)
300 ml (½ pint) milk
6 large shelled scallops
salt and pepper

▪

1 PUT the butter or margarine and onion into a large bowl. Cover and cook on HIGH for 5–7 minutes until the onion is very soft, stirring occasionally.

▪

2 MEANWHILE, wash the watercress. Reserve a few sprigs for garnishing and chop the remainder.

▪

3 ADD the flour to the onion and cook on HIGH for 1 minute, stirring once. Gradually stir in the stock and half the milk, then add the chopped watercress. Cook on HIGH for 7–8 minutes until boiling and thickened, stirring occasionally.

▪

4 To prepare the scallops, if necessary, remove and discard the tough white 'muscle' from each scallop (found opposite the coral). Separate the corals from the scallops. Slice the white part into three discs.

▪

5 ARRANGE the scallops and corals in a shallow dish. Pour over the remaining milk and cook on HIGH for 1–2 minutes or until the scallops look opaque. Pour the milk into the soup.

▪

6 POUR the soup into a blender or food processor and purée until smooth. Season to taste with salt and pepper. Return the purée to the rinsed-out bowl, then cook on HIGH for 2 minutes or until hot.

▪

7 POUR the soup into six soup bowls, add three pieces of scallop and one coral to each bowl. Garnish with the reserved watercress and serve immediately.

Sweet Cooked Clams (page 50)

CHINESE MUSHROOM AND CRAB BROTH

Shiitake mushrooms are a tree fungus, grown in China and Japan then dried by the sun or artificial heat. They have a good flavour, but need to be soaked in warm water before using. If you cannot find them use cup or flat black mushrooms instead.

SERVES 4

8 dried Chinese (Shiitake) mushrooms
45 ml (3 tbsp) soy sauce
30 ml (2 tbsp) white vinegar
15 ml (1 tbsp) sesame or vegetable oil
2.5 cm (1 inch) piece fresh root ginger, peeled and thinly sliced

1 red chilli, seeded and sliced
15 ml (1 level tbsp) cornflour
175 g (6 oz) cooked fresh or canned crab meat
4 spring onions, trimmed and sliced

1 SOAK the dried Chinese mushrooms in warm water for 30 minutes. Drain and cut in half.

2 PUT the soy sauce, vinegar, oil, ginger and chilli into a medium bowl with 600 ml (1 pint) water. Cover and cook on HIGH for 5–6 minutes or until boiling.

3 BLEND the cornflour with a little cold water to make a smooth paste, then gradually stir into the soup. Cook on HIGH for 2–3 minutes until boiling and thickened, stirring occasionally. Add the crab meat, spring onions and mushrooms and mix well.

4 COVER and cook on HIGH for 3–4 minutes until thoroughly heated through. Serve immediately.

CHILLED SKATE AND LEMON SOUP

An unusual soup to serve in the summer, and ideal for entertaining as it can be made in advance and chilled before serving.

SERVES 6

1 skate wing, weighing about 450 g (1 lb)
1 medium onion, skinned and grated
2 celery sticks, grated
1 carrot, grated
finely grated rind and juice of 1 large lemon

1 bay leaf
300 ml (½ pint) milk
salt and pepper
150 ml (¼ pint) soured cream
15 ml (1 tbsp) black lumpfish roe
lemon shreds, to garnish

1 PUT the skate in a large bowl and sprinkle with the onion, celery, carrot, lemon rind and juice and the bay leaf. Pour over 300 ml (½ pint) water, cover and cook on HIGH for 5–6 minutes or until the fish begins to flake away from the bone.

■

2 REMOVE the fish from the bowl. Discard the skin and bone and place the flaked fish in a blender or food processor. Meanwhile, continue to cook the vegetables on HIGH, covered, for 6–8 minutes or until tender. Cool slightly, then add to the blender with the cooking liquid and the milk. Purée until smooth, then season to taste with salt and pepper.

■

3 RETURN the soup to the rinsed-out bowl and chill for at least 3 hours before serving.

■

4 SERVE with the soured cream and lumpfish roe swirled through. Sprinkle with the lemon shreds to garnish.

■ THICK PRAWN AND VEGETABLE SOUP ■

This slightly spicy soup is substantial enough for a light meal if served with lots of crusty bread.

SERVES 6

15 ml (1 tbsp) olive oil
1 medium onion, skinned and chopped
1 garlic clove, skinned and crushed
5–10 ml (1–2 tsp) sweet chilli sauce (optional)
3 tomatoes, chopped
1 green chilli, seeded and chopped (optional)
5 ml (1 level tsp) dried oregano

1 medium potato, peeled and finely diced
50 g (2 oz) long grain rice
450 ml (¾ pint) milk
75 g (3 oz) frozen petit pois
1 green pepper, seeded and finely chopped
225 g (8 oz) cooked peeled prawns
salt and pepper

■

1 PUT the oil, onion, garlic, chilli sauce, tomatoes, chilli, oregano, potato, rice and 450 ml (¾ pint) boiling water into a large bowl. Cover and cook on HIGH for 10–12 minutes or until the vegetables are softened, stirring occasionally.

■

2 ADD the milk, re-cover and cook on HIGH for 10–12 minutes or until the rice is tender.

■

3 ADD the peas, pepper and prawns and season to taste with salt and pepper. Cover and cook on HIGH for 3–4 minutes. Serve immediately.

· *JAPANESE CLEAR SOUP WITH PRAWNS* ·

Japanese soups are often made with a seaweed-based stock, to give a delicate flavour.

SERVES 4

15 g (½ oz) dried seaweed, such as kombu, wakame or nori
15 ml (1 tbsp) soy sauce
4 raw jumbo prawns in the shell

2 medium carrots
5 cm (2 inch) piece daikon radish
15 ml (1 tbsp) sake or dry sherry
4 slices of lime

·

1 PUT the seaweed, soy sauce and 900 ml (1½ pints) boiling water into a large bowl. Cover and cook on HIGH for 3 minutes or until the water returns to the boil, then cook on HIGH for a further 5 minutes.

·

2 MEANWHILE, remove the shells from the prawns, leaving the tail intact (see page 13). Then, using kitchen scissors or a sharp knife, cut along the curved underside of the prawn from the thick end towards the tail, stopping at the tail and being careful not to cut the prawn through completely.

·

3 FLATTEN out the prawns and remove and discard the veins. Cut a slit in the middle of the prawn and curl the tail round and push it through the slit.

·

4 PEEL the carrots and daikon radish and cut into thin slices or decorative shapes.

·

5 REMOVE and discard the seaweed from the stock. Stir the sake or sherry, carrots and daikon radish into the stock. Cover and cook on HIGH for 3 minutes, then add the prawns and continue to cook for 2 minutes or until the prawns are cooked.

·

6 USING a slotted spoon, transfer the fish and vegetables to four soup bowls, then carefully pour over the stock. Add a slice of lime to each bowl and serve immediately.

· *LOBSTER BISQUE* ·

Live lobster must never be cooked in the microwave, so ask your fishmonger to cook it for you or follow the instructions on page 12 for conventional cooking.

SERVES 6

1 large lobster, cooked
2 carrots, scrubbed and sliced
1 medium onion, skinned and sliced
1 celery stick, chopped
2 parsley sprigs
1 bay leaf
1 litre (1¾ pints) fish stock

25 g (1 oz) butter or margarine
25 g (1 oz) plain flour
150 ml (¼ pint) dry white wine
15 ml (1 tbsp) brandy (optional)
150 ml (¼ pint) double cream
salt and pepper
fleurons, to garnish

·

1 SCRUB the lobster shell thoroughly. Cut the lobster in half and remove the tail meat. Crack the claws and remove the meat (see page 13).

·

2 CUT the meat into neat pieces, save a few pieces for the garnish and put the remainder into a large bowl. Break up the lobster shell and put into the bowl. Add the carrots, onion, celery, parsley, bay leaf and 600 ml (1 pint) of the stock. Cover and cook on HIGH for 5 minutes or until boiling, then cook on HIGH for 25–30 minutes or until the vegetables are very soft.

·

3 PUT the butter or margarine, flour, wine and remaining stock into a large bowl and cook on HIGH for 6–7 minutes until boiling and thickened, stirring occasionally.

·

4 STRAIN the lobster stock into the thick sauce. Return the lobster meat, shell and vegetables to the bowl and pound together, using the end of a rolling pin until the vegetables are well mashed. Return to the sieve and push through into the rest of the soup. Add the brandy and cream and season with salt and pepper.

·

5 COOK on HIGH for 2–3 minutes or until hot but not boiling. Serve immediately, garnished with the reserved lobster meat and fleurons.

· STARTERS ·

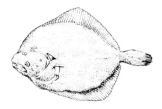

Fish is always a popular choice for a starter, whether smoked, marinated, in a salad or made into a hot dish. A starter is served at the beginning of a meal to whet your appetite, so it is important that the food looks attractive as well as tasting good. For this reason, most of the recipes in this chapter also give suggestions for simple garnishes. They really are worth experimenting with as they make a great deal of difference to the visual appeal of a dish.

If serving a hot main course it is sensible to serve a cold first course that can be prepared in advance, and vice versa. When choosing a starter, it is also worth considering whether the main course is very substantial and therefore needs only a light starter such as Butterfly Prawns, or whether it can happily follow something more filling like Fresh Pasta with Courgettes and Smoked Trout.

· FILO TRIANGLES WITH TWO FILLINGS ·

Filo pastry, sometimes spelt phyllo, is a paper-thin pastry made of flour and water. It is possible to make it at home but it is a time-consuming task because of the amount of rolling and stretching needed to make it really thin, so buy it ready prepared and keep it in the freezer. Thaw before using.

SERVES 6

75 g (3 oz) butter or margarine
4 sheets of packet filo pastry, each measuring about 45.5×28 cm (18×11 inches)
75 ml (5 tbsp) natural yogurt
15 ml (1 tbsp) tahini
15 ml (1 tbsp) lemon juice
¼ of a cucumber
lemon wedges, to garnish

CRAB, WALNUT AND GINGER FILLING
40 g (1½ oz) cooked crab meat, flaked
25 g (1 oz) walnut halves, very finely chopped

2.5 cm (1 inch) piece root ginger, peeled and finely grated
15 ml (1 tbsp) lemon juice
salt and pepper

PRAWN, CREAM CHEESE AND DILL FILLING
75 g (3 oz) cooked peeled prawns, roughly chopped
50 g (2 oz) cream cheese
10 ml (2 tsp) chopped fresh dill
10 ml (2 tsp) lemon juice

1 To make the two fillings, mix the crab, walnut and ginger ingredients together in one bowl and the prawn, cream cheese and dill ingredients in another bowl. Season each filling to taste with salt and pepper.

■

2 PUT the butter or margarine into a small bowl and cook on HIGH for 2 minutes or until melted.

■

3 LAY one sheet of pastry on top of a second sheet and cut widthways into six 7.5 cm (3 inch) strips. (Keep the remaining pastry covered with a damp tea towel or it will dry out and crack.)

■

4 BRUSH the strips of pastry with the melted butter or margarine. Place a teaspoon of the crab filling at one end of each strip of pastry. Fold the pastry diagonally across the filling to form a triangle. Continue folding keeping the triangle shape, until you reach the end of the strip of pastry. Repeat with the remaining strips of pastry.

■

5 HEAT a browning dish on HIGH for 5–8 minutes or according to the manufacturer's instructions.

■

6 WHILE the browning dish is heating, repeat steps 3 and 4 with the remaining pastry and the prawn filling to make a total of twelve filo triangles. Brush both sides of each triangle with melted butter or margarine.

■

7 USING tongs, quickly add six triangles to the dish and cook on HIGH for 1–2 minutes until the underside of each triangle is golden brown and the top looks puffy. Turn over and cook on HIGH for 1–2 minutes until the second side is golden brown.

■

8 REHEAT the browning dish on HIGH for 2–3 minutes, then repeat with the remaining triangles.

■

9 WHILE the filo triangles are cooking, make the sauce. Put the yogurt, tahini and lemon juice in a bowl and mix together. Grate in the cucumber and season to taste with salt and pepper.

■

10 SERVE the filo traingles warm or cold, garnished with lemon wedges, with the sauce handed separately.

CRAB AND CASHEW NUT SAUTÉ WITH GLUTINOUS RICE BALLS ▪

Glutinous rice is a gluten free rice used in Chinese cooking. There are two varieties, white which is dehulled in processing or the black kind as used here. It has a pleasant nutty texture, and a slightly sticky texture once cooked. It is available from Chinese supermarkets and some health food shops.

SERVES 4

100 g (4 oz) black glutinous rice
15 ml (1 tbsp) vegetable oil
15 ml (1 level tbsp) paprika
2.5 ml (½ level tsp) ground turmeric
75 g (3 oz) shelled cashew nuts
30 ml (2 tbsp) hoisin sauce

30 ml (2 tbsp) lemon juice
225 g (8 oz) cooked white crab meat (see page 13)
few Chinese leaves
shredded spring onions, to garnish

▪

1 To make the rice balls, put the rice and 300 ml (½ pint) boiling water into a large bowl. Cover and cook on HIGH for 12–14 minutes until the rice is tender and the water is absorbed, stirring frequently.

▪

2 USING a wooden spoon, beat the rice vigorously until it just starts to cling together. While the rice is still warm, shape it into twelve small balls. Set aside while heating the crab.

▪

3 PUT the oil in a browning dish or a large bowl and cook on HIGH for 1 minute or until hot. Add the paprika and turmeric, stirring well, then cook on HIGH for 1 minute.

▪

4 ADD the cashews and stir to coat in the oil. Cook on HIGH for 2–3 minutes until the cashews are lightly browned, stirring once.

▪

5 STIR in the hoisin sauce and the lemon juice. Flake the crab meat and stir into the sauce. Cook on HIGH for 2–3 minutes or until heated through, stirring occasionally.

▪

6 REHEAT the rice balls on HIGH for 1–2 minutes or until hot.

▪

7 MEANWHILE, arrange one or two Chinese leaves on four serving plates, and spoon the crab and cashew sauté on top. Place three rice balls on each plate. Serve immediately, garnished with the spring onions.

▪ *TURBOT AND PISTACHIO TIMBALES* ▪

Turbot has the perfect flavour and texture for these timbales, but it can be difficult to find at the fishmongers and it is expensive. If you cannot buy turbot, try using another firm white fish instead (see below).

SERVES 4

397 g (14 oz) can tomatoes
30 ml (2 tbsp) dry white wine
salt and pepper
225 g (8 oz) turbot or firm white fish
   fillet such as cod, haddock, monkfish
   or hake, skinned
1 egg white

15 ml (1 tbsp) lemon juice
300 ml (½ pint) Greek strained yogurt
   or double cream
15 ml (1 level tbsp) chopped fresh dill
25 g (1 oz) shelled pistachio nuts,
   chopped
dill and pistachio nuts, to garnish

▪

1 To make the sauce, put the tomatoes and wine into a large bowl. Break up the tomatoes with a spoon and season generously with salt and pepper. Cook on HIGH for 12 minutes or until reduced and thickened.

▪

2 MEANWHILE, roughly chop the turbot and put into a blender or food processor with the egg white and lemon juice. Purée until smooth.

▪

3 WITH the machine still running, gradually add the yogurt or the cream. Mix in the chopped dill and nuts, then season to taste with salt and pepper.

▪

4 SPOON the fish mixture into four greased 150 ml (¼ pint) ramekin dishes and level the surfaces. Cover each with a piece of greaseproof paper. Arrange in a circle in the cooker and cook on MEDIUM for 6–8 minutes or until the timbales feel firm to the touch.

▪

5 WHILE the timbales are cooking, pass the tomato mixture through a sieve to make a smooth sauce. Season to taste with salt and pepper.

▪

6 CAREFULLY unmould the timbales on to four plates. Reheat the sauce on HIGH for 1–2 minutes until hot and spoon on to the plates. Garnish with dill and a few pistachio nuts, then serve immediately.

· TROUT WITH RASPBERRY VINAIGRETTE ·

This makes a lovely summer starter. If you want to serve four, then simply double the ingredients and cook the fish on HIGH for 3–5 minutes or until tender. The dressing and the fish can be prepared in advance and the whole thing assembled just before serving.

SERVES 2

2 trout fillets, each weighing about
   100 g (4 oz)
30 ml (2 tbsp) fish or vegetable stock or
   water (see pages 125 and 123)
100 g (4 oz) raspberries

30 ml (2 tbsp) nut or olive oil
pinch of sugar
mixed salad leaves, such as radicchio,
   endive, lamb's lettuce, red lalola

·

1 CUT each trout fillet in half widthways and arrange them in a single layer in a shallow dish. Pour over the fish or vegetable stock or water. Cover and cook on HIGH for 1½–2 minutes or until the fish is cooked. Leave to cool.

·

2 RESERVE a few raspberries for the garnish, purée the remainder in a blender or food processor, then push through a sieve to remove the pips. Whisk half the oil and the sugar into the raspberry purée.

·

3 TEAR the salad leaves into small pieces, toss in the remaining oil and arrange on two plates with the cold trout. Spoon over the raspberry vinaigrette and serve immediately.

· FRESH PASTA WITH COURGETTES AND SMOKED TROUT ·

Fresh pasta cooks very quickly and the time will depend on the size and shape. The timings in this recipe are for tagliatelle; if using shapes such as shells increase the time by 30 seconds–1 minute.

SERVES 4 AS A STARTER OR 2 AS A MAIN COURSE

2 medium courgettes
15 ml (1 tbsp) olive oil
pinch of saffron
225 g (8 oz) fresh spinach pasta, such
   as tagliatelle
salt and pepper

1 smoked trout, weighing about 225 g
   (8 oz)
150 ml (¼ pint) crème fraîche or double
   cream
30 ml (2 tbsp) black lumpfish roe
fresh herb sprigs, to garnish

·

1 CUT the courgettes into very thin diagonal slices. Cut each slice in half. Put the courgettes, oil and saffron into a medium bowl and cook on HIGH for 1 minute, stirring once.

2 PUT the fresh spinach pasta and salt to taste into a large bowl. Pour over enough boiling water to cover by at least 2.5 cm (1 inch) and cook on HIGH for 1–1½ minutes or until almost tender. Leave to stand while finishing the sauce. Do not drain.

■

3 To finish the sauce, remove and discard the skin and bones from the trout. Flake the flesh and stir into the courgettes with the crème fraîche or cream and salt and pepper to taste. Cook on HIGH for 2 minutes until hot and slightly thickened.

■

4 DRAIN the pasta and return to the large bowl. Pour over the sauce and toss together to mix. If necessary, reheat the sauce and pasta together on HIGH for about 2 minutes. Transfer the pasta to four plates, top each with a spoonful of lumpfish roe and garnish with a herb sprig.

■ *BUTTERFLY PRAWNS* ■

Butterfly prawns are prawns that have been cut down the middle and opened out like the wings of a butterfly. It helps them to cook quickly and looks very attractive.

SERVES 4

8 raw jumbo prawns
15 ml (1 tbsp) vegetable oil
1 garlic clove, skinned and crushed
1 small green chilli, seeded and
   chopped (optional)

2.5 cm (1 inch) piece fresh root ginger,
   peeled and grated
2 spring onions, trimmed and sliced
30 ml (2 tbsp) soy sauce
30 ml (2 tbsp) dry sherry

■

1 HEAT a browning dish on HIGH for 5–8 minutes or according to the manufacturer's instructions.

■

2 MEANWHILE, remove the shells from the prawns, leaving the tail intact, then using kitchen scissors or a sharp knife, cut along the curved underside of the prawn from the thick end towards the tail, stopping at the tail and being careful not to cut the prawn through completely.

■

3 FLATTEN out the prawns and remove and discard the veins.

■

4 ADD the oil to the browning dish, then quickly add the prawns, cut side down. Cook on HIGH for 1½ minutes, then turn over and cook on HIGH for a further 1½–2 minutes or until the prawns are bright red in colour and the flesh looks opaque.

■

5 TRANSFER the prawns to a serving dish. Stir the remaining ingredients into the browning dish and cook on HIGH for 1 minute or until hot, stirring once. Pour over the fish and serve immediately.

· STUFFED MUSSELS WITH PINE NUTS AND RAISINS ·

Don't be put off at the thought of spending hours stuffing mussels. It won't take as long as you think and is well worth the effort. As they are served cold they can be made in advance.

SERVES 4

30 ml (2 tbsp) olive oil
1 large onion, skinned and finely
  chopped
50 g (2 oz) rice
5 ml (1 level tsp) ground allspice
cayenne pepper
salt and pepper
50 g (2 oz) pine nuts
50 g (2 oz) raisins

30 ml (2 tbsp) chopped fresh parsley or
  coriander
150 ml (¼ pint) dry white wine
2.5 ml (½ level tsp) ground turmeric
700 g (1½ lb) fresh mussels, cleaned
  (see page 12)
30 ml (2 tbsp) Greek strained yogurt
chopped fresh parsley or coriander, to
  garnish

■

1 To make the stuffing, put the oil, onion, rice, allspice and cayenne pepper to taste into a medium bowl and cook on HIGH for 2 minutes, stirring once. Add salt to taste and pour over 150 ml (¼ pint) boiling water. Cover and cook on HIGH for 10–12 minutes until the water is absorbed and the rice is tender.

■

2 STIR in the pine nuts, raisins and parsley or coriander and season to taste with pepper and more salt if necessary. Leave to cool.

■

3 PUT the wine and turmeric into a large bowl and cook on HIGH for 1 minute. Add the mussels, cover and cook on HIGH for 3–5 minutes or until all of the mussels have opened, removing the mussels on the top as they open and shaking the bowl occasionally. Discard any mussels which do not open.

■

4 DRAIN the mussels in a sieve, reserving the cooking liquid.

■

5 RETURN the cooking liquid to the large bowl and cook on HIGH for 8–10 minutes until reduced by half. Stir in the yogurt and season to taste with salt and pepper. Leave to cool.

■

6 MEANWHILE, reserve four mussels for the garnish, then discard one half of the shell from the remainder. Stuff the mussels with the rice stuffing. The easiest way to do this is to use each mussel to scoop up the filling.

■

7 To serve, arrange the mussels on four plates, then pour the sauce around them. Garnish with the reserved mussels and sprigs of parsley or coriander. Serve with Hot Lemon and Herb Bread (see page 120).

· SPINACH, MUSSEL AND MUSHROOM SALAD ·

This colourful starter can be made a few hours in advance up to step 6 and then assembled just before serving. Remove some of the mussels from their shells after cooking, if wished.

SERVES 4

1 large yellow or red pepper
45 ml (3 tbsp) olive oil
1 small onion, skinned and finely
   chopped
4 large flat black mushrooms, sliced
700 g (1½ lb) mussels, cleaned (see
   page 12)

150 ml (¼ pint) dry white wine
salt and pepper
175 g (6 oz) fresh spinach, washed and
   trimmed

·

1 PRICK the pepper all over with a fork and rub with a little of the oil. Lay on a piece of absorbent kitchen paper and cook on HIGH for about 3–4 minutes until just soft, turning over once.

·

2 LEAVE to cool slightly, then cut the flesh into neat cubes, discarding the seeds and the core.

·

3 PUT the remaining oil, onion and mushrooms into a large bowl. Cover and cook on HIGH for 3–4 minutes or until the mushrooms are cooked, stirring once. Using a slotted spoon, remove the mushrooms and add to the cubes of pepper.

·

4 ADD the wine and the mussels to the onion and oil. Cover and cook on HIGH for 3–5 minutes until all of the mussels have opened, removing the mussels on the top as they open and shaking the bowl occasionally. Discard any mussels which do not open.

·

5 DRAIN the mussels in a sieve, reserving the liquid, and mix with the mushrooms and pepper. Return the cooking liquid to the bowl and cook, uncovered, on HIGH for 8–10 minutes until reduced by half.

·

6 LEAVE the cooking liquid to cool. Season to taste with salt and pepper, then pour over the mussels, mushrooms and peppers and mix together.

·

7 TEAR any large spinach leaves into two or three pieces and arrange on four plates. Pour over the mussel mixture and toss lightly together. Serve at once.

▪ *NORI-WRAPPED FISH* ▪

This recipe is based on a Japanese speciality called sushi which basically consists of rice flavoured with vinegar wrapped in nori, which is a kind of seaweed (available from Oriental and wholefood shops). Although fiddly, it is well worth making and looks most attractive if garnished with a selection of colourful vegetables cut into decorative shapes.

SERVES 4

150 g (5 oz) short grain white rice
15 ml (1 tbsp) white wine vinegar
15 ml (1 tbsp) soy sauce
15 ml (1 tbsp) dry sherry
15 ml (1 tbsp) sugar
15 ml (1 tbsp) creamed horseradish
cayenne pepper
225 g (8 oz) flat white fish fillets, such as whiting, plaice or sole

30 ml (2 tbsp) milk
salt and pepper
2 sheets of nori, each measuring about 18×20.5 cm (7×8 inches)
½ a small cucumber
50 g (2 oz) button mushrooms
2 medium carrots
black and red lumpfish roe, to garnish (optional)

▪

1 PUT the rice into a large bowl and pour over 350 ml (12 fl oz) boiling water. Cover and cook on HIGH for 8–10 minutes or until the rice is tender and all the water is absorbed.

▪

2 PUT the vinegar, soy sauce, sherry and sugar into a small bowl and cook on HIGH for 1–2 minutes or until hot. Stir until the sugar is dissolved. Stir in the horseradish and cayenne pepper to taste, then pour the mixture over the rice and mix with a fork so that all the rice is coated in sauce. Leave to cool.

▪

3 WHILE the rice is cooling, put the fish into a shallow dish and pour over the milk. Cover and cook on HIGH for 2–3 minutes or until the fish flakes easily. Flake the fish, discarding the skin and cooking liquid. Leave to cool.

▪

4 WHEN the rice is cool, season to taste with salt and pepper. (It should have a fairly sticky consistency.) Lay the two sheets of nori on a flat surface and spread the cold rice in an even layer over three quarters of each piece of nori, taking it right to the edges.

▪

5 FINELY chop half the cucumber and the mushrooms. Sprinkle the cucumber, mushrooms and flaked fish on top of the rice.

▪

6 CAREFULLY roll up the nori, starting from the rice covered-edge (holding the ingredients in place at first if necessary) to make two fat cylinders. Wrap tightly and chill in the refrigerator for at least 30 minutes.

▪

7 MEANWHILE, cut flower, fish and other decorative shapes from the remaining cucumber and the carrots.

8 To serve, cut each cylinder into six slices, using a sharp wet knife. Arrange the slices on four plates, garnish with the vegetable shapes and lumpfish roe and serve immediately.

▪ *FISH TERRINE WITH TOMATO AND BASIL SAUCE* ▪

This is a perfect starter to make in the summer when there is an abundance of fresh basil.

SERVES 6

16 large basil leaves
700 g (1½ lb) white fish fillets, such as cod, haddock, monkfish or sole, skinned
2 eggs
150 ml (¼ pint) double cream

150 ml (¼ pint) Greek strained yogurt
15 ml (1 tbsp) lemon juice
salt and pepper
4 tomatoes, skinned and seeded
10 ml (2 tsp) tomato purée

▪

1 GREASE a 1.1 litre (2 pint) ring mould and line the base with about 12 of the basil leaves.

▪

2 ROUGHLY chop the fish and purée in a blender or food processor until smooth. With the machine still running, gradually add 1 egg and the white from the remaining egg, half the cream, half the yogurt and the lemon juice. Season to taste with salt and pepper.

▪

3 CAREFULLY spoon the fish mixture into the greased mould and level the surface. Cover with a piece of greaseproof paper and cook on MEDIUM for 8–10 minutes or until firm to the touch. Leave to stand for 10 minutes.

▪

4 UNCOVER and place a wire rack over the top of the mould. Invert the rack and mould on to a baking tray or shallow dish to catch the liquid that will run out of the mould. Leave to drain for about 5 minutes, then turn over again so that the terrine is still in the mould and the rack is on top. Remove the rack, then unmould the terrine on to a plate. Leave to cool.

▪

5 To make the sauce, put the tomatoes, remaining cream and yogurt, egg yolk and tomato purée in a blender or food processor and process until smooth. Cook on LOW for 3–4 minutes, until slightly thickened, stirring occasionally. Leave to cool.

▪

6 To serve, cut the terrine into slices and arrange on six serving plates, with a little of the sauce. Finely slice the remaining basil leaves and scatter over the sauce. Serve immediately.

▪ FRIED FISH PARCELS WITH WARM CARROT AND MANGE TOUT SALAD ▪

Don't worry if the paper chars as you fry the parcels, but make sure that you don't leave the microwave unattended while they are cooking.

SERVES 4

30 ml (2 tbsp) walnut or vegetable oil
5–10 ml (1–2 tsp) sweet chilli sauce
30 ml (2 tbsp) soy sauce
30 ml (2 tbsp) dry sherry
700 g (1½ lb) firm white fish fillets
  such as haddock, cod or monkfish,
  skinned

175 g (6 oz) mange tout
175 g (6 oz) carrots, scrubbed
salt and pepper

▪

1 PUT half the oil, the chilli sauce, soy sauce and sherry into a bowl and mix together. Cut the fish into twelve 5 cm (2 inch) cubes, and add to the sauce. Stir so that all the fish is coated and leave for 30 minutes to marinate.

▪

2 MEANWHILE, top and tail the mange tout and cut the carrots into very thin strips about 5 cm (2 inches) long. Put the vegetables into a medium bowl with the remaining oil and season to taste with salt and pepper. Cover and set aside.

▪

3 HEAT a browning dish on HIGH for 5–8 minutes or according to the manufacturer's instructions.

▪

4 WHILE the browning dish is heating, cut twelve pieces of greaseproof paper measuring about 30.5 cm (12 inches) by 61 cm (24 inches). Fold each piece in half widthways to make a 30.5 cm (12 inch) square.

▪

5 REMOVE the fish from the marinade and place a piece on each square of paper. Fold the paper over the fish to completely enclose it and make a neat parcel.

▪

6 PUT the parcels in a single layer in the browning dish and cook on HIGH for 3 minutes. Turn over and cook on HIGH for 2 minutes or until the fish is cooked. (Carefully open one parcel to check that the fish is cooked.) Remove the browning dish from the cooker and set aside. (Leave the parcels in the browning dish to keep warm).

▪

7 COOK the vegetables on HIGH for 1–2 minutes or until just warm. Arrange on four large plates, then place the fish parcels on top. Serve immediately.

Leaf-wrapped Mullet (page 78)
Lime and Hake Kebabs with Tabouleh (page 55)

▪ SMOKED MACKEREL AND APPLE MOUSSE WITH HORSERADISH MAYONNAISE ▪

This slightly sweet fish mousse combines very well with the sharp, tangy horseradish mayonnaise.

SERVES 6

225 g (8 oz) cooking apples
1 small onion, skinned and chopped
4 smoked mackerel fillets
30 ml (2 tbsp) creamed horseradish
75 ml (5 tbsp) mayonnaise
15 ml (1 level tbsp) gelatine

60 ml (4 tbsp) lemon juice
salt and pepper
3 red skinned eating apples
few sprigs of watercress or flat leaf
   parsley
45 ml (3 tbsp) natural yogurt

▪

1 PEEL and finely chop the cooking apples and put into a medium bowl with the onion. Cover and cook on HIGH for 5–7 minutes or until the apples and onion are very soft, stirring occasionally. Leave to cool slightly.

▪

2 MEANWHILE, flake the mackerel and put into a blender or food processor with half the creamed horseradish and 30 ml (2 tbsp) of the mayonnaise. Process for about 1 minute or until well mixed.

▪

3 WHEN the apple mixture has cooled, add to the mackerel in the blender and process until almost smooth.

▪

4 PUT the gelatine, 15 ml (1 tbsp) of the lemon juice and 15 ml (1 tbsp) water into a small bowl. Cook on HIGH for 30 seconds, do not allow to boil. Stir until dissolved, then add to the mackerel and apple purée.

▪

5 SEASON to taste with salt and pepper, then spoon into six greased ramekin dishes. Chill in the refrigerator for at least 2 hours or until set.

▪

6 To serve, core, quarter and slice the eating apples, mix with the watercress or parsley and toss in 30 ml (2 tbsp) of the lemon juice. Season with salt and pepper. Arrange the salad on six plates.

▪

7 DIP the mousses briefly in hot water, then unmould on to the plates. Mix the yogurt with the remaining creamed horseradish, mayonnaise and lemon juice. Season with salt and pepper and serve with the mousses.

Egg Noodles with Squid, Shrimps and Almonds (page 59)

· SWEET COOKED CLAMS ·

Clams make a pretty and unusual starter. Make sure that you use small venus clams, rather than any of the much larger varieties.

SERVES 2

450 g (1 lb) venus clams in the shell
2.5 cm (1 inch) piece of fresh root ginger, peeled and grated
60 ml (4 tbsp) sake or dry sherry
15 ml (1 level tbsp) caster sugar

45 ml (3 tbsp) soy sauce
10 ml (2 level tsp) cornflour
2.5 cm (1 inch) piece of cucumber
1 spring onion, trimmed

1 THOROUGHLY scrub the clams.

2 PUT the ginger, sake or sherry, sugar and soy sauce into a large bowl and cook on HIGH for 2–3 minutes or until hot. Stir until the sugar is dissolved. Blend the cornflour with 60 ml (4 tbsp) water and stir into the sauce. Cook on HIGH for 2 minutes or until boiling and thickened, stirring once.

3 ADD the clams and stir to coat in the sauce. Cook on HIGH for 4–5 minutes or until the clams have opened, stirring occasionally. Discard any clams which do not open.

4 MEANWHILE, cut the cucumber and onion into very thin strips.

5 SPOON the clams and sauce on to two plates. Sprinkle with the cucumber and spring onion and serve immediately.

· SMOKED EEL PÂTÉ ·

Smoked eel has a pleasant, rich buttery texture and an earthy flavour. It is an excellent choice for a pâté.

SERVES 6

175 g (6 oz) smoked eel
75 g (3 oz) butter
15 ml (1 tbsp) lemon juice

10 ml (2 tsp) creamed horseradish
45 ml (3 tbsp) soured cream
salt and pepper

1 REMOVE and discard the skin and backbone from the eel and roughly chop the flesh.

2 CUT the butter into small pieces, put into a small bowl and cook on HIGH for 1–2 minutes or until melted. Cool slightly.

3 WHILE the butter is cooling, put the lemon juice and the eel into a blender or food processor and purée until smooth. Add the butter and process until well mixed.

■

4 ADD the horseradish, soured cream and salt and pepper to taste. Process briefly until mixed, then turn into a serving dish. Serve at room temperature with Melba toast.

■ *HERB AND PARMESAN-STUFFED SQUID* ■

Squid are very easy to prepare following the instructions on page 11, but if you still find them daunting, ask your fishmonger to prepare them for you.

SERVES 4

75 g (3 oz) fresh breadcrumbs
45 ml (3 tbsp) chopped fresh mixed herbs
30 ml (2 level tbsp) grated Parmesan cheese
salt and pepper
1 egg, beaten
2 medium squid, each weighing about 225 g (8 oz) cleaned (see page 11)

225 g (8 oz) tomatoes, skinned, seeded and finely chopped
3 anchovies, chopped
150 ml (¼ pint) dry white wine
150 ml (¼ pint) fish or vegetable stock (see pages 125 and 123)
fresh herbs, to garnish

■

1 To make the stuffing, mix together the breadcrumbs, herbs, Parmesan cheese and salt and pepper in a bowl. Add the egg and mix together to bind.

■

2 FILL the squid bodies with the stuffing mixture. Thread a trussing needle with fine string and carefully sew up each pouch.

■

3 PUT the tomatoes, anchovies, wine, stock and seasoning into a large bowl. Add the stuffed squid, and the tentacles, cut into 5 cm (2 inch) pieces. Cover and cook on MEDIUM for 10–12 minutes or until tender.

■

4 REMOVE the squid. Cook the cooking liquid on HIGH for 8–10 minutes until reduced by half.

■

5 RETURN the squid to the reduced sauce and cook on HIGH for 2–3 minutes to reheat.

■

6 To serve, spoon the sauce on to four plates. Remove the string from the squid and cut into thin slices. Arrange on the plates with the tentacles. Garnish with fresh herbs and serve immediately.

▪ MINIATURE MONKFISH KEBABS ON A SPINACH PURÉE ▪

Monkfish has a firm, meaty texture that is perfect for kebabs.

SERVES 4

450 g (1 lb) monkfish, skinned
15 ml (1 level tbsp) coriander seeds
5 ml (1 level tsp) ground cardamom
3 limes
15 ml (1 tbsp) vegetable oil

salt and pepper
450 g (1 lb) fresh spinach or 226 g
  (8 oz) packet frozen spinach
45 ml (3 tbsp) Greek strained yogurt

▪

1 REMOVE and discard the central bone and cut the fish into twenty-four 2 cm (¾ inch) cubes, then put into a shallow dish. Crush the coriander seeds and mix with the cardamom. Add the finely grated rind and juice of 1 lime, the oil and salt and pepper.

▪

2 POUR the spice mixture over the fish and mix so that all the fish is coated. Cover and leave to marinate for 20–30 minutes.

▪

3 MEANWHILE, peel and slice the remaining limes and set aside.

▪

4 REMOVE any tough stems from the fresh spinach, chop roughly and put into a bowl. Cover and cook on HIGH for 5–6 minutes until tender, stirring once. If using frozen spinach, put into a bowl, cover and cook on HIGH for 7–8 minutes, until thawed, stirring frequently. Drain thoroughly.

▪

5 PURÉE the spinach in a blender or food processor until smooth, then stir in the yogurt and season to taste with salt and pepper. Return to the bowl.

▪

6 THREAD the monkfish on to twelve wooden cocktail sticks, putting two pieces on each stick. Arrange in a single layer in the shallow dish containing the marinade. Cover and cook on HIGH for 2½–3½ minutes until just tender, rearranging once.

▪

7 POUR the cooking liquid from the fish into the spinach purée and cook on HIGH for 1–2 minutes or until hot. Spoon on to four plates. Arrange three kebabs on each plate on top of the purée. Garnish with the lime slices and serve immediately.

· LIGHT FISH DISHES ·

Light fish dishes are perfect served for lunch or as a light evening meal. Some, such as Lime and Hake Kebabs with Tabouleh, or Egg Noodles with Squid, Shrimps and Almonds are balanced meals in themselves; others need little accompaniment other than a mixed or green salad.

For a more substantial meal you could consider serving a filling starter such as pasta, soup or a coarse terrine or pâté and follow with a dish from this chapter. Other recipes in this chapter as Jumbo Prawns with Garlic and Brandy, Poppy Seed Prawns on Poppadums or Cockles and Leeks in Pastry Cases are equally delicious served as starters.

· HADDOCK WITH YOGURT, SPICES AND DRIED FRUITS ·

This is a particularly light fish dish – and it's low in calories and high in fibre too.

SERVES 4

6 no-soak dried apricots
4 dried dates, stoned
2.5 ml (½ level tsp) ground turmeric
5 ml (1 level tsp) ground mixed spice
pinch of ground chilli

450 g (1 lb) haddock fillets, skinned
30 ml (2 tbsp) milk
60 ml (4 tbsp) natural yogurt
salt and pepper

·

1 CUT the apricots and dates in half and put into a bowl with the spices and 200 ml (7 fl oz) water. Cover and cook on HIGH for 6–7 minutes or until the fruit is soft, stirring occasionally.

·

2 CUT the fish into four neat pieces and put into a shallow dish with the milk. Cover and cook on HIGH for 3–4 minutes or until cooked. Strain the milk into the softened dried fruits. Transfer the fish to four serving plates.

·

3 ADD the yogurt to the dried fruits and season to taste with salt and pepper. Cook on HIGH for 1–2 minutes until hot. Spoon over the fish and serve immediately.

▪ FISH-STUFFED JACKET POTATOES ▪

Jacket potatoes are wonderfully quick to cook in the microwave and make a tasty meal when stuffed with a mixture of fish and cheese.

SERVES 2–4

2 medium potatoes, weighing about
   200 g (7 oz) each
225 g (8 oz) fish fillets, such as cod,
   haddock or coley
30 ml (2 tbsp) milk
65 g (2½ oz) cream cheese with herbs
   and garlic

30 ml (2 tbsp) chopped fresh mixed
   herbs, such as parsley, chives or dill
salt and pepper
50 g (2 oz) Cheddar cheese, grated

▪

1 PRICK the potatoes all over, place on a piece of absorbent kitchen paper and cook on HIGH for 8–10 minutes until tender, turning once.

▪

2 PUT the fish into a shallow dish and pour over the milk. Cover and cook on HIGH for 2–3 minutes or until the fish flakes easily.

▪

3 WHILE the fish is cooking, cut the potatoes in half and scoop out the flesh, leaving a shell about 0.5 cm (¼ inch) thick. Mash the potato with the cream cheese and the herbs.

▪

4 WHEN the fish is cooked, remove and discard the skin and flake the flesh. Mix the flaked fish and any milk remaining after cooking with the potato. Season to taste with salt and pepper.

▪

5 PILE the potato mixture back into the potato skins and arrange on a plate. Cook on HIGH for 2–3 minutes until hot.

▪

6 SPRINKLE with the cheese and cook on HIGH for 1 minute until melted. Serve hot with a mixed salad.

▪ MACKEREL WITH MINT ▪

Mackerel and mint are a delicious combination – and the mint fills the kitchen with a wonderful aroma during cooking.

SERVES 2

2 small mackerel, each about 225 g
   (8 oz), cleaned
salt and pepper
small bunch of fresh mint
1 lemon

½ a cucumber
15 ml (1 tbsp) olive oil
150 ml (¼ pint) crème fraîche, soured
   cream or Greek strained yogurt
mint sprigs, to garnish

1 REMOVE the heads from the mackerel but leave the tails intact. Wash the fish then season generously inside and out with salt and pepper.

∎

2 STUFF the fish with some of the mint leaves. Make two slashes on each side of the fish. Put into a shallow dish and squeeze the lemon juice all over the fish. Cover and cook on HIGH for 5–6 minutes until tender.

∎

3 WHILE the fish is cooking, cut the cucumber into strips about 4 cm (1½ inches) long and 0.5 cm (¼ inch) wide and put into a bowl with the oil. Roughly chop the remaining mint and mix with the cucumber. Mix in the crème fraîche, soured cream or yogurt and season to taste.

∎

4 ARRANGE the cooked fish on two plates. Cook the cucumber on HIGH for 2–3 minutes until just warm. Arrange on the plates around the mackerel. Garnish with mint sprigs and serve immediately.

∎ *LIME AND HAKE KEBABS WITH TABOULEH* ∎

Tabouleh is a salad of Lebanese origin. It is based on burghul or cracked wheat and contains masses of fresh mint and parsley, so it has lots of flavour and combines very well with hake which tends to lack flavour.

SERVES 4

175 g (6 oz) burghul
700 g (1½ lb) hake fillets, skinned
2 limes
60 ml (4 tbsp) chopped fresh parsley
60 ml (4 tbsp) chopped fresh mint

finely grated rind and juice of 1 lemon
2 small red onions, skinned and very finely chopped
45 ml (3 tbsp) olive oil
salt and pepper

∎

1 PUT the burghul into a bowl and pour over 300 ml (½ pint) boiling water. Leave to soak for 10–15 minutes until all the water is absorbed.

∎

2 MEANWHILE, cut the hake into 2.5 cm (1 inch) cubes. Thinly slice one and a half of the limes. Thread the lime slices and the hake on to four bamboo skewers. Arrange the kebabs in a single layer in a large shallow dish. Squeeze the juice from the remaining half lime over the kebabs.

∎

3 PUT the burghul into a bowl and mix with the parsley, mint, lemon rind and juice, onions and oil. Season generously with salt and pepper. Arrange on four plates.

∎

4 COVER the kebabs and cook on HIGH for 4–5 minutes or until the fish is cooked, re-positioning the kebabs once during cooking. Arrange the kebabs on top of the tabouleh and serve at once.

· FISH BALLS IN A WALNUT SAUCE ·

This is an unusual way of serving bland fish. Be careful when rearranging the fish balls in step 5 or they will break up. Serve the fish balls with a rice pilaff.

Serves 4

450 g (1 lb) white fish fillets, such as
    haddock, cod or whiting
30 ml (2 tbsp) milk
50 g (2 oz) fresh brown breadcrumbs
1 small onion, skinned and very finely
    chopped
30 ml (2 tbsp) chopped fresh coriander
    or parsley
salt and pepper
1 egg yolk

100 g (4 oz) walnut halves
2 garlic cloves, skinned and crushed
5 ml (1 level tsp) paprika
5 ml (1 level tsp) ground coriander
pinch of ground cloves
30 ml (2 tbsp) white wine vinegar
450 ml (¾ pint) fish or vegetable stock
    (see pages 125 and 123)
walnut halves and coriander or parsley
    sprigs, to garnish

1 PUT the fish into a shallow dish with the milk. Cover and cook on HIGH for 4–5 minutes until the fish flakes easily. Flake the fish, discarding the skin and any bones. Reserve the cooking liquid.

2 PUT the fish, breadcrumbs, onion, fresh coriander or parsley and salt and pepper to taste into a blender or food processor and purée until smooth. Gradually add the egg yolk to bind the mixture together to make a fairly stiff consistency.

3 SHAPE the mixture into 20 walnut-size balls. Chill while making the sauce.

4 PUT the walnuts, garlic, paprika, ground coriander, cloves and vinegar into the rinsed-out bowl of the blender or food processor and purée until smooth. Transfer to a large bowl and cook on HIGH for 2 minutes, stirring frequently.

5 ADD the reserved cooking liquid and the stock to the walnut mixture and cook on HIGH for 5–6 minutes or until boiling, stirring once. Carefully add the fish balls and cook on MEDIUM for 5–6 minutes or until they feel firm to the touch, rearranging once during cooking. Garnish with walnut halves and coriander or parsley sprigs and serve hot with a rice pilaff.

· COD WITH WATERCRESS SAUCE ·

If you don't have a browning dish, put the fish in a shallow dish with 30 ml (2 tbsp) milk, cover and cook on HIGH for 4–5 minutes or until cooked.

SERVES 2

1 small bunch of watercress
30 ml (2 tbsp) natural yogurt
5 ml (1 tsp) lemon juice
5 ml (1 level tsp) mild mustard
1 egg yolk
salt and pepper

75 ml (5 tbsp) vegetable oil
2 cod steaks, each weighing about
   175 g (6 oz)
15 ml (1 level tbsp) plain flour
15 g (½ oz) butter or margarine

■

1 WASH and trim the watercress. Reserve a few sprigs for garnish, then put the rest into a large bowl with 15 ml (1 tbsp) water. Cover and cook on HIGH for 1 minute or until the watercress looks slightly limp.

■

2 DRAIN the watercress and let it cool a little, then purée in a blender or food processor with the yogurt. Set aside.

■

3 HEAT a browning dish on HIGH for 5–8 minutes or according to the manufacturer's instructions.

■

4 MEANWHILE, put half the lemon juice, the mustard, egg yolk and salt and pepper to taste into a medium bowl. Whisk together, then gradually whisk in the oil, a little at a time, until the mixture becomes thick and creamy.

■

5 WHEN all the oil has been added, add the remaining lemon juice and more seasoning if necessary. Fold in the watercress purée and set aside.

■

6 LIGHTLY coat the fish with the flour and season with salt and pepper. Put the butter or margarine into the browning dish and swirl to coat the base of the dish, then quickly add the fish. Cook on HIGH for 2 minutes, then turn over and cook on HIGH for 1–2 minutes or until tender. Transfer to two plates.

■

7 COOK the watercress sauce on HIGH for 1 minute or until warm, stirring occasionally. Pour over the fish, garnish with the reserved watercress sprigs and serve immediately.

· FISH GOUJONS ·

Serve these tasty goujons as soon as they are cooked or they will become soggy and flavourless.

SERVES 2

450 g (1 lb) sole or plaice fillets, skinned
5 ml (1 level tsp) dried thyme
5 ml (1 level tsp) dried marjoram
30 ml (2 level tbsp) sesame seeds
60 ml (4 level tbsp) plain flour

finely grated rind of 1 small lemon
salt and pepper
30 ml (2 tbsp) milk
30 ml (2 tbsp) vegetable oil
lemon wedges, to garnish

■

1 CUT the fish into strips about 0.5 cm (¼ inch) wide and 7.5 cm (3 inches) long.

■

2 HEAT a browning dish on HIGH for 5–8 minutes or according to the manufacturer's instructions.

■

3 MEANWHILE, mix the thyme, marjoram, sesame seeds, flour and lemon rind together. Season generously with salt and pepper.

■

4 COAT the strips of fish in the milk, then toss in the herb and flour mixture. When the browning dish is hot, add the oil then the goujons.

■

5 COOK on HIGH for 30 seconds, then carefully stir the fish and cook on HIGH for 1 minute or until the fish is just cooked. Serve the fish immediately, garnished with lemon wedges.

· STUFFED SPRATS ·

Sprats are part of the herring family but much smaller and usually eaten whole. For this recipe you will need the largest sprats you can buy.

SERVES 4

12 large sprats, cleaned and scaled
100 g (4 oz) full fat soft cheese
1 garlic clove, skinned and crushed
30 ml (2 tbsp) chopped fresh mixed herbs, such as parsley, thyme and sage

salt and pepper
finely grated rind and juice of 1 lemon

■

1 MAKE two slashes on each side of the fish and remove the heads if desired. Wash thoroughly.

2 To make the stuffing, mix the cheese, garlic and half the herbs together and season to taste with salt and pepper. Add enough lemon juice to thin the mixture slightly.

■

3 FILL the fish cavities with the stuffing and arrange in a single layer in a large shallow dish. Pour over the remaining lemon juice.

■

4 COVER and cook on HIGH for 4–5 minutes or until the fish are cooked. Season generously with pepper, sprinkle with the remaining herbs and the lemon rind and serve immediately.

■ *EGG NOODLES WITH SQUID, SHRIMPS AND ALMONDS* ■

There are many different types of noodles available. This recipe uses a packet of the kind sold as Chinese egg noodles.

SERVES 4–6

250 g (9 oz) packet thin egg noodles
45 ml (3 tbsp) hoisin sauce
15 ml (1 tbsp) lemon juice
30 ml (2 tbsp) soy sauce
15 ml (1 tbsp) sweet chilli sauce
45 ml (3 tbsp) sesame oil
30 ml (2 tbsp) vegetable oil
1 garlic clove, skinned and crushed
450 g (1 lb) squid, cleaned (see page 11)

50 g (2 oz) blanched almonds
100 g (4 oz) cooked peeled shrimps or prawns
100 g (4 oz) beansprouts
3 spring onions, trimmed and roughly chopped
black pepper
shredded lettuce and lemon wedges, to garnish

■

1 PUT the noodles into a large bowl and pour over about 1.7 litres (3 pints) boiling water or enough to cover the noodles. Cover and cook on HIGH for 2 minutes. Leave to stand while cooking the fish.

■

2 PUT the hoisin sauce, lemon juice, soy sauce, chilli sauce, oils and garlic into a large bowl. Cut the squid into small pieces or rings and mix into the sauce with the almonds. Cook on HIGH for 5 minutes or until the squid just looks opaque, stirring once.

■

3 ADD the shrimps or prawns, beansprouts and drained noodles and mix thoroughly together. Cover and cook on HIGH for 2–3 minutes or until hot, stirring once. Stir the spring onions into the noodle mixture. Season to taste with black pepper.

■

4 To serve, spoon on to plates and top each portion with a pile of shredded lettuce and a lemon wedge. Serve immediately.

• WARM SALAD OF SALMON AND SCALLOPS •

Although both salmon and scallops are expensive, this salad makes a little of each go a long way.

SERVES 4

225 g (8 oz) salmon steak or cutlet
8 large shelled scallops
selection of salad leaves such as curly
    endive, Webb's wonder lettuce,
    radicchio and watercress
2 stale bridge rolls
45 ml (3 tbsp) olive or nut oil

45 ml (3 tbsp) crème fraîche or soured
    cream
10 ml (2 level tsp) wholegrain mustard
15 ml (1 tbsp) lemon juice
salt and pepper
a few chopped fresh herbs such as
    parsley, chives, dill and tarragon

■

1 SKIN the salmon and remove the bone, if necessary. Cut across the grain into very thin strips. If necessary, remove and discard from each scallop the tough white 'muscle' which is found opposite the coral. Separate the corals from the scallops. Slice the scallops into three or four pieces vertically. Cut the corals in half if they are large.

■

2 HEAT a browning dish on HIGH for 5–8 minutes or according to the manufacturer's instructions.

■

3 MEANWHILE, tear the salad leaves into small pieces, if necessary, and arrange on four plates. Cut the rolls into thin slices.

■

4 ADD 30 ml (2 tbsp) of the oil to the browning dish and swirl to coat the bottom of the dish. Quickly add the sliced rolls and cook on HIGH for 2 minutes. Turn over and cook on HIGH for a further 1 minute or until crisp. Remove from the dish and set aside.

■

5 ADD the remaining oil and the scallops, corals and salmon to the dish and cook on HIGH for 1½ minutes or until the fish looks opaque, stirring once.

■

6 USING a slotted spoon, remove the fish from the dish, and arrange on top of the salad leaves.

■

7 PUT the crème fraîche or soured cream, mustard, lemon juice and salt and pepper to taste into the browning dish and cook on HIGH for 1–2 minutes or until hot. Stir thoroughly and pour over the fish. Sprinkle with the croûtons and herbs and serve immediately.

· PRAWN AND SESAME PARCELS WITH BEANSPROUT SALAD ·

These parcels are rather like Chinese Dim Sum — they are fun to make and delicious to eat.

SERVES 2

15 ml (1 tbsp) vegetable oil
50 g (2 oz) button mushrooms, chopped
1 cm (½ inch) piece of fresh root ginger, peeled and grated
2 spring onions, trimmed and finely chopped
75 g (3 oz) cooked peeled prawns

20 ml (4 tsp) soy sauce
100 g (4 oz) strong plain wholemeal flour
15 ml (1 tbsp) sesame seeds
salt and pepper
1 egg yolk
25 g (1 oz) beansprouts
1.25 ml (¼ level tsp) five-spice powder

■

1 PUT the oil, mushrooms, ginger, spring onions, prawns and half the soy sauce into a medium bowl. Cook on HIGH for 2 minutes or until the mushrooms are softened.

■

2 PUT the flour into a bowl and add the sesame seeds and salt and pepper to taste. Make a well in the centre, then add the egg yolk and about 30 ml (2 tbsp) cold water to make a soft dough.

■

3 KNEAD the dough lightly, then roll out on a lightly floured surface to a 30.5 cm (12 inch) square. Cut into four squares, then divide the filling between them. Brush the edges of the pastry with water, then bring the four points of each square together to form an envelope-shaped parcel, and press to seal.

■

4 PUT the parcels on to two small plates. Divide the beansprouts between the two plates. Mix the remaining soy sauce with the five-spice powder and drizzle over the beansprouts.

■

5 COVER each plate and cook on HIGH for 4–5 minutes or until the parcels are just 'set' and feel firm to the touch. Serve immediately.

▪ *SAG PRAWNS* ▪

This favourite Indian dish converts well to microwave cooking.

SERVES 4

*900 g (2 lb) fresh spinach or 450 g
(1 lb) frozen leaf spinach
45 ml (3 tbsp) vegetable oil
1 small onion, skinned and finely
chopped
1 garlic clove, skinned and crushed
10 ml (2 level tsp) ground ginger*

*10 ml (2 level tsp) garam masala
5 ml (1 level tsp) mustard seeds
2.5 ml (½ level tsp) chilli powder
2.5 ml (½ level tsp) ground turmeric
450 g (1 lb) cooked peeled prawns
60 ml (4 tbsp) desiccated coconut
salt and pepper*

▪

1 REMOVE any tough stems from the fresh spinach, chop roughly and put into a bowl. Cover and cook on HIGH for 8–10 minutes until tender, stirring once. If using frozen spinach, put into a bowl, cover and cook on HIGH for 10–12 minutes, until thawed, stirring frequently. Drain thoroughly.

▪

2 PUT the oil, onion, garlic, ginger, garam masala, mustard seeds, chilli powder and turmeric into a bowl. Cover and cook on HIGH for 4–5 minutes until the onion is softened.

▪

3 ADD the prawns and stir to coat in the spicy oil. Add half the coconut, the spinach and season to taste with salt and pepper. Cover and cook on HIGH for 4–5 minutes, stirring occasionally. Serve immediately, sprinkled with the remaining coconut.

▪ *JUMBO PRAWNS WITH GARLIC AND BRANDY* ▪

*Large raw prawns are available at fishmongers and some Chinese stores.
You can use smaller prawns if you wish, but the dish will not look quite so
spectacular.*

SERVES 4

*12 raw jumbo prawns in the shell
25 g (1 oz) butter
30 ml (2 tbsp) olive oil
2 garlic cloves, skinned and crushed*

*15 ml (1 tbsp) brandy
15 ml (1 tbsp) chopped fresh parsley
salt and pepper*

▪

1 To prepare the prawns, remove the legs, leaving the shell and tail intact. Using kitchen scissors or a sharp knife, cut along the curved underside of the prawn from the thick end towards the tail and carefully remove the vein.

2 PUT the butter, oil and garlic into a large shallow dish and cook on HIGH for 2 minutes until the butter is melted.

■

3 ADD the prawns in a single layer and cook on HIGH for 4–5 minutes until the prawns turn bright pink in colour, stirring occasionally.

■

4 SPRINKLE the brandy and parsley over the prawns and season to taste with salt and pepper. Serve immediately.

■ *POPPY SEED PRAWNS ON POPPADUMS* ■

Poppadums are very easy to cook in the microwave and save time, even though only one is cooked at a time.

SERVES 4

4 poppadums
30 ml (2 tbsp) vegetable oil
1 garlic clove, skinned and crushed
5 ml (1 level tsp) ground turmeric
5 ml (1 level tsp) ground coriander
1.25 ml (¼ level tsp) ground chilli

15 ml (1 level tbsp) black poppy seeds
397 g (14 oz) can tomatoes
175 g (6 oz) cooked peeled prawns
30 ml (2 tbsp) chopped fresh coriander
salt and pepper
fresh coriander, to garnish

■

1 BRUSH each poppadum on one side with a little of the oil. Cook one at a time on HIGH for 1 minute or until crisp and puffed up all over.

■

2 PUT the remaining oil and the garlic, turmeric, ground coriander, ground chilli and poppy seeds into a medium bowl and cook on HIGH for 1 minute. Add the tomatoes and mash with a fork to break them up. Cook on HIGH for 5–6 minutes until the liquid is slightly reduced.

■

3 ADD the prawns and fresh coriander, season to taste with salt and pepper and cook on HIGH for 1½–2 minutes until the prawns are heated through.

■

4 To serve, put the poppadums on four plates and spoon the prawns on top. Garnish with coriander and serve immediately.

▪ COCKLES AND LEEKS IN PASTRY CASES ▪

*The unusual combination of cockles and creamed leeks makes a tasty filling
for these delicate, crisp pastry shells.*

SERVES 4

100 g (4 oz) plain wholemeal flour
5 ml (1 level tsp) dried mustard
  powder
5 ml (1 level tsp) paprika
salt and pepper
75 g (3 oz) butter or margarine
450 g (1 lb) leeks

45 ml (3 tbsp) soured cream or Greek
  yogurt
300 ml (½ pint) cooked shelled cockles
  (see chart on page 14)
60 ml (4 level tbsp) grated Parmesan
  cheese

▪

1 PUT the flour, mustard powder, paprika and a pinch of salt into a
bowl. Rub in 50 g (2 oz) of the butter or margarine until the mixture
resembles fine breadcrumbs. Add about 45–60 ml (3–4 tbsp) water and
mix together with a round-bladed knife to form a dough.

▪

2 ROLL out thinly on a lightly floured surface and divide into four pieces.
Use to cover the base and sides of four inverted 10 cm (4 inch)
round shallow glass flan dishes. Cover and chill while making the filling.

▪

3 To make the filling, put the remaining butter or margarine into a bowl
and cook on HIGH for 1 minute until melted.

▪

4 TRIM and finely chop the leeks, then rinse thoroughly to remove any
grit. Add to the melted butter, cover and cook on HIGH for 8–10 minutes
until really soft. Stir in the cream or yogurt, cockles, half the Parmesan
cheese and season to taste with salt and pepper.

▪

5 To cook the pastry cases, prick them all over with a fork and cook,
pastry side uppermost, on HIGH for 2½–3 minutes until the pastry feels
firm to the touch. Carefully unmould the pastry cases and place on four
plates.

▪

6 COOK the leek and cockle filling on HIGH for 2 minutes until hot,
stirring once. Carefully spoon into the pastry cases, sprinkle with the
remaining Parmesan cheese and serve immediately.

Opposite: *Warm Salad of Salmon and Scallops (page 60)*
Overleaf: *Plait of Salmon and Courgettes (page 74)*

· *SPAGHETTI ALLE VONGOLE* ·

Spaghetti is the usual pasta to serve with this clam and tomato sauce, but use shapes such as shells or bows if you prefer.

SERVES 4

397 g (14 oz) can tomatoes
10 ml (2 tsp) tomato purée
45 ml (3 tbsp) olive oil
1–2 garlic cloves, skinned and crushed
150 ml (¼ pint) dry white wine
350 g (12 oz) spaghetti

900 g (2 lb) venus clams, cleaned (see page 12)
45 ml (3 tbsp) chopped fresh parsley
salt and pepper
grated Parmesan cheese, to serve

1 PUT the tomatoes, tomato purée, oil, garlic and wine into a large bowl. Cook on HIGH for 12–14 minutes until reduced and slightly thickened. Set aside while cooking the pasta.

2 PUT the spaghetti into a large bowl and pour over enough boiling water to cover the pasta by about 2.5 cm (1 inch). Cover and cook on HIGH for 7–10 minutes or until almost tender. Leave to stand while cooking the clams. Do not drain.

3 STIR the clams and parsley into the sauce. Cover and cook on HIGH for 4–6 minutes until the clams have opened, stirring occasionally. Discard any clams which have not opened.

4 DRAIN the spaghetti and toss with the sauce. Season to taste with salt and pepper. Serve immediately with grated Parmesan cheese.

Previous page: *Fish with Coriander Masala (page 75)*
Opposite: *Stuffed Herrings (page 76)*

· Main Course Fish Dishes ·

This chapter contains recipes using a wide variety of fish, from the everyday Potato-topped Fish Pie using fillets of cod, haddock or coley to the more exotic Grey Mullet with Pomegranates or Conger Eel Stew.

As some of the more unusual fish are not always available throughout the country, I have given alternatives, although in the case of certain fish such as conger eel or carp this is not possible. It is important to buy whichever fish is freshest and then go home and decide what to cook with it, rather than to go shopping with the intention of buying a particular fish even if it is not in prime condition. Always buy fresh fish in preference to frozen (see the notes in the introduction on buying fresh fish).

· *FISH IN A FLASH ON A PLATE* ·

What could be simpler – a perfectly cooked fish, microwaved and served on the same plate? As flat fish cooks very quickly in the microwave, set your timer for 2 minutes to begin with, check the fish and then set the timer for a further 1–2 minutes. A 450 g (1 lb) flat fish will only take about 3 minutes to cook.

Serves 1–2

25 g (1 oz) butter or margarine or
*   flavoured butter (see page 122)*
1 whole flat fish, such as sole or plaice,
*   weighing about 450 g (1 lb), cleaned*

lemon juice
salt and pepper

·

1 Smear half the butter or margarine on a plate which is the same size as the fish. Lay the fish on top of the butter and spread with the remainder.

·

2 Using a sharp knife, cut two or three large slashes across the fish. Sprinkle with lemon juice.

·

3 Invert a plate on top of the fish to cover it completely. Cook on HIGH for 3–4 minutes or until the fish is cooked. Remove the top plate, season with salt and pepper and serve immediately.

▪ *FISHY PIES* ▪

Ready-made puff pastry puffs up like magic in the microwave but it doesn't go brown. These fish shaped pies are sprinkled with Parmesan, parsley and paprika to give them some colour. Serve them with a green vegetable.

SERVES 4

*370 g (13 oz) packet ready-to-roll puff
  pastry, thawed
300 ml (½ pint) milk
30 ml (2 tbsp) grated Parmesan cheese
30 ml (2 tbsp) chopped fresh parsley
paprika
50 g (2 oz) butter or margarine*

*50 g (2 oz) plain flour
15 ml (1 tbsp) mild wholegrain mustard
450 g (1 lb) white fish fillets, such as
  cod, haddock, sole or coley, skinned
75 g (3 oz) mature Cheddar cheese
salt and pepper*

▪

1 CUT the pastry into four. Roll each piece out thinly on a lightly floured surface to a rectangle about 20.5×18 cm (8×7 inches).

▪

2 CUT a large fish shape from each rectangle. Brush with a little of the milk. Mix the Parmesan cheese and parsley together and sprinkle on the pastry. Season with a little paprika. Prick all over with a fork.

▪

3 PLACE one of the 'fishes' on a double sheet of absorbent kitchen paper and cook on HIGH for 2–3 minutes or until puffed up all over. Do not open the door during cooking or the pastry will collapse.

▪

4 REPEAT with the remaining 'fishes'.

▪

5 PUT the butter or margarine, flour, mustard and milk into a bowl and cook on HIGH for 4–5 minutes or until boiling and thickened, stirring frequently.

▪

6 CUT the fish fillets into small pieces and stir into the sauce. Cook on HIGH for 3–4 minutes or until the fish is tender, stirring once.

▪

7 ADD the Cheddar cheese and season to taste with salt and pepper. Cook on HIGH for 1 minute to melt the cheese.

▪

8 CUT the pastry 'fishes' in half horizontally and place the bottom halves on four plates. Spoon over the fish mixture. Replace the top halves and serve immediately with a green vegetable.

▪ SOLE AND SPINACH ROULADES ▪

Serve three of these pretty spinach-filled roulades per person.

SERVES 4

12 sole fillets, each weighing about 75 g
  (3 oz), skinned
5 ml (1 level tsp) fennel seeds, lightly
  crushed
salt and pepper

12 spinach or sorrel leaves, washed
15 ml (1 tbsp) dry white wine
45 ml (3 tbsp) Greek strained yogurt
pinch of ground turmeric

▪

1 PLACE the sole fillets, skinned side up, on a chopping board. Sprinkle with the fennel seeds and season to taste with salt and pepper. Lay a spinach or sorrel leaf, vein side up on top of each fillet, then roll up and secure with a wooden cocktail stick.

▪

2 ARRANGE the fish in a circle around the edge of a large shallow dish and pour over the wine. Cover and cook on HIGH for 6–7 minutes or until tender.

▪

3 REMOVE the fish from the cooking liquid, using a slotted spoon, and transfer to a serving plate.

▪

4 GRADUALLY stir the yogurt and turmeric into the cooking liquid. Season to taste with salt and pepper and cook on HIGH for 1–2 minutes until slightly thickened, stirring occasionally. Serve the roulades with a little of the sauce poured over.

▪ FISH WITH MUSTARD SEEDS ▪

Mustard seeds give this dish a subtle flavour and an attractive speckled appearance. Serve with green beans.

SERVES 4

45 ml (3 level tbsp) black mustard seeds
900 g (2 lb) firm white fish fillets, such
  as monkfish, cod, hake, turbot,
  haddock, skinned
30 ml (2 level tbsp) plain flour
30 ml (2 tbsp) vegetable oil
1 medium onion, skinned and thinly
  sliced

1 garlic clove, skinned and crushed
150 ml (¼ pint) Greek yogurt or soured
  cream
15 ml (1 tbsp) lemon juice
30 ml (2 tbsp) chopped fresh coriander
salt and pepper
whole unpeeled prawns and parsley
  sprigs, to garnish

▪

1 PUT the mustard seeds in a bowl with 60 ml (4 tbsp) water and leave to soak while cooking the fish.

2 HEAT a browning dish on HIGH for 5–8 minutes or according to the manufacturer's instructions.

■

3 MEANWHILE, cut the fish into 2.5 ml (1 inch) cubes and toss in the flour.

■

4 WHEN the browning dish is hot, add the oil, onion and garlic and cook on HIGH for 2 minutes or until the onion is softened, stirring once.

■

5 ADD the fish and cook on HIGH for 2 minutes, then turn over and cook for a further 1–2 minutes or until the fish is cooked.

■

6 ADD the yogurt or cream, lemon juice and mustard seeds and coriander and cook on HIGH for 2–3 minutes until boiling and slightly thickened, stirring occasionally, but being careful not to break up the fish. Season to taste with salt and pepper, then garnish with the prawns and parsley and serve with green beans.

■ *FISH WITH HAZELNUT SAUCE* ■

Do not overcook the hazelnuts or the sauce will have a bitter, burnt flavour.

SERVES 4

100 g (4 oz) hazelnuts
4 white fish steaks, such as haddock or cod, each weighing about 175 g (6 oz)
45 ml (3 tbsp) dry white wine, fish or vegetable stock (see pages 125 and 123)

150 ml (¼ pint) double cream or Greek strained yogurt
salt and pepper
ground mace
watercress, to garnish

■

1 SPREAD the hazelnuts out on a large plate and cook on HIGH for 6–8 minutes until lightly browned. Tip on to a clean tea towel and rub off the loose brown skin then chop finely.

■

2 ARRANGE the fish in a single layer in a large shallow dish and pour over the wine or stock. Cover and cook on HIGH for 6–7 minutes or until the fish is cooked.

■

3 TRANSFER the fish to a serving dish.

■

4 PUT the hazelnuts and cream or yogurt into the cooking dish and cook on HIGH for 2 minutes until hot. Season to taste with salt, pepper and mace, then pour over the fish. Garnish with watercress and serve immediately.

▪ *POTATO-TOPPED FISH PIE* ▪

This is a basic recipe for fish pie which can be varied with the addition of peeled prawns, mushrooms, grated cheese, or fresh herbs of your choice.

SERVES 4

700 g (1½ lb) potatoes
450 g (1 lb) white fish fillets, such as
    cod, haddock or coley
225 g (8 oz) smoked haddock
450 ml (¾ pint) milk
50 g (2 oz) butter or margarine

salt and pepper
25 g (1 oz) plain flour
grated nutmeg
2 hard-boiled eggs, shelled
45 ml (3 tbsp) chopped fresh parsley

▪

1 PEEL the potatoes and cut them into 0.5 cm (¼ inch) slices. Put into a large bowl with 45 ml (3 tbsp) water.

▪

2 PUT the fish in a single layer in a large shallow dish with 30 ml (2 tbsp) of the milk. Cover and place on top of the bowl containing the potatoes. Put both dishes into the cooker and cook on HIGH for 8–9 minutes or until the fish flakes easily.

▪

3 REMOVE the fish from the cooker. Stir the potatoes, re-cover and continue to cook on HIGH for about 10 minutes or until tender.

▪

4 WHILE the potatoes are cooking, strain the cooking liquid from the fish into a medium bowl and reserve. Remove and discard the skin and any bones from the fish. Flake the fish and put into a flameproof and microwaveproof serving dish.

▪

5 WHEN the potatoes are cooked, mash with half of the butter or margarine and about 75 ml (5 tbsp) of the milk or enough to make soft mashed potato. Season to taste with salt and pepper.

▪

6 PUT the remaining milk, butter or margarine and flour into the bowl with the reserved cooking liquid and cook on HIGH for 4–5 minutes or until boiling and thickened, whisking frequently. Season to taste with salt, pepper and nutmeg. Roughly chop the hard-boiled eggs and stir into the sauce with the parsley. Pour over the fish.

▪

7 SPOON or pipe the mashed potato on top of the fish mixture. Cook on HIGH for 4–5 minutes or until the pie is hot, then brown under a hot grill if desired. Serve at once with a green vegetable.

· *FISH SATAY* ·

*Satay is a popular Indonesian dish. Skewers of meat or fish are marinated
and then cooked and served with a spicy peanut sauce.*

Serves 4

*900 g (2 lb) thick firm white fish fillets,
  such as cod, haddock, monkfish,
  hake or huss, skinned
30 ml (2 tbsp) vegetable oil
2 garlic cloves, skinned and crushed
45 ml (3 tbsp) soy sauce
30 ml (2 tbsp) lemon juice
10 ml (2 level tsp) dark soft brown
  sugar*

*2.5 ml (½ level tsp) ground ginger
5 ml (1 level tsp) ground coriander
2.5 ml (½ level tsp) cayenne pepper
75 ml (5 level tbsp) crunchy peanut
  butter
50 g (2 oz) creamed coconut
2.5 ml (½ level tsp) chilli powder
½ a cucumber
paprika*

1 Cut the fish into 2.5 cm (1 inch) cubes and put into a large shallow
dish.

2 Mix the oil, garlic, soy sauce, lemon juice, sugar, ginger, coriander and
cayenne together and pour over the fish. Stir the fish until it is all coated
in the marinade. Cover and leave to marinate in a cool place for
2–3 hours or overnight, stirring the fish occasionally.

3 To make the peanut sauce, put the peanut butter and the creamed
coconut in a medium bowl. Pour over 150 ml (¼ pint) boiling water and
stir to break up the coconut. Cook on HIGH for 1–2 minutes if the
coconut will not dissolve. Stir in the chilli powder.

4 To cook the fish, remove from the marinade and thread on to eight
bamboo skewers. Arrange in the dish containing the marinade and cook
on HIGH for 4–5 minutes or until the fish is cooked, carefully
rearranging once and basting with the marinade during cooking.

5 While the fish is cooking, cut the cucumber into small neat wedges,
sprinkle with a little paprika and arrange on a serving plate.

6 When the fish is cooked, arrange it on the serving platter with the
cucumber. Pour any remaining marinade into the peanut sauce and cook
on HIGH for 1–2 minutes or until hot. Serve with the fish.

▪ FISH IN CREAM AND WINE SAUCE ▪

This simple sauce transforms cod or haddock into something special.

SERVES 4

1 shallot, skinned and finely chopped
25 g (1 oz) butter or margarine
1 bay leaf
150 ml (¼ pint) dry white wine
4 white fish cutlets, such as cod or
    haddock, each weighing about 225 g
    (8 oz)

45 ml (3 tbsp) double cream
salt and pepper
chopped fresh parsley, to garnish

▪

1 PUT the shallot, butter or margarine and bay leaf into a large shallow dish. Cover and cook on HIGH for 3–4 minutes or until the shallot is soft, stirring occasionally.

▪

2 ADD the wine and cook on HIGH for 5–6 minutes or until the wine is reduced by half.

▪

3 DISCARD the bay leaf and arrange the fish in a single layer in the dish. Cover and cook on HIGH for 6–7 minutes or until the fish is tender. Remove the fish and arrange on four plates.

▪

4 STIR the cream into the sauce and cook on HIGH for 2–3 minutes or until boiling and slightly reduced. Season to taste with salt and pepper. Pour over the fish, garnish with parsley and serve immediately.

▪ FISH WITH GREEN LENTILS ▪

Cutting the fish in a criss-cross pattern not only makes it look more attractive, but helps it to cook more quickly too.

SERVES 4

225 g (8 oz) green lentils, washed
bouquet garni
3 large tomatoes, roughly chopped
1 garlic clove, skinned and crushed
30 ml (2 tbsp) olive oil
3 allspice berries, crushed
salt and pepper

4 small whole fish such as trout, red
    mullet, mackerel or herring, each
    weighing about 225 g (8 oz), scaled
    and cleaned
lemon wedges and fresh herbs, to
    garnish

▪

1 PUT the lentils and bouquet garni into a medium bowl and pour over enough boiling water to cover the lentils by about 2.5 cm (1 inch). Cover and cook on HIGH for 10–15 minutes or until the lentils are just tender.

2 DRAIN the lentils and return to the rinsed-out bowl with the tomatoes, garlic, half the oil, the allspice and salt and pepper to taste.

■

3 USING a sharp knife, make deep cuts in a criss-cross pattern on each side of the fish, then arrange in a single layer in a large shallow dish. Brush with the remaining oil.

■

4 COVER the fish and place on top of the bowl containing the lentils. Place both dishes in the cooker and cook on HIGH for about 10 minutes or until the fish is tender, rearranging the fish once during cooking.

■

5 ARRANGE the lentils on four plates with the fish. Garnish with lemon wedges and fresh herbs and serve immediately.

■ *ANCHOVY AND GARLIC STUFFED MONKFISH* ■

Monkfish is very expensive, but makes delicious eating. For a more economical dish substitute rockfish (also known as huss or dogfish), a much cheaper fish which like monkfish has a central bone and no smaller bones.

SERVES 4

50 g (2 oz) can anchovies in olive oil
3 garlic cloves, skinned and crushed
45 ml (3 tbsp) chopped fresh parsley
finely grated rind and juice of ½ a lemon

black pepper
1.4 kg (3 lb) piece of monkfish, skinned
parsley sprigs and lemon slices, to garnish

■

1 PUT the anchovies and the oil from the can, the garlic, parsley, lemon rind and juice into a blender or food processor and purée until smooth. Season to taste with black pepper.

■

2 LAY the fish on a large double sheet of greaseproof paper, then spread the anchovy and garlic paste over the top and the sides. Carefully roll the fish up inside the paper. Twist the ends together so that the paper is firmly wrapped around the fish. (This will ensure that the moisture is retained during cooking.)

■

3 PLACE the fish in a large shallow dish and cook on HIGH for 12–14 minutes or until the fish is cooked (open the parcel and check the fish after 12 minutes).

■

4 To serve, unwrap the fish and place on a serving platter. Pour the cooking juice around the fish, garnish with parsley and lemon slices and serve immediately.

▪ *PLAIT OF SALMON AND COURGETTES* ▪

This stunning dish is surprisingly easy to prepare. It is ideal for a special occasion as the plaiting can be prepared in advance.

SERVES 4

150 ml (¼ pint) dry white vermouth
large pinch of saffron strands
75 g (3 oz) butter or margarine
150 ml (¼ pint) double cream

3 large long courgettes
900 g (2 lb) piece of fresh salmon, cut from the middle
salt and pepper

▪

1 PUT the vermouth and saffron into a medium bowl and cook on HIGH for 2–3 minutes until just boiling. Add 50 g (2 oz) of the butter or margarine and the cream and cook on HIGH for 4–5 minutes until slightly thickened. Set aside while cooking the fish.

▪

2 TOP and tail the courgettes, then cut lengthways into 0.5 cm (¼ inch) slices. Cut the green outer slices into thin strips and add to the sauce. You will need twelve middle slices to make the plaits. If you have more, cut them into thin strips and add to the sauce.

▪

3 CUT the salmon either side of the central bone to make two pieces. To remove the skin, put the fish, skin side down on a flat board. Starting at one corner of the thinner end insert a sharp knife between the skin and the flesh. Using a sawing action, carefully remove the skin, keeping the flesh in one piece. Repeat with the second piece of salmon. Discard the skin and the bone.

▪

4 CUT the salmon against the grain into twelve neat strips about 1.5 cm (¾ inch) wide. Cut the four thickest strips in half horizontally to make sixteen equal-sized strips.

▪

5 REMOVE the turntable from the cooker and cover with a double sheet of greaseproof paper. (If your cooker does not have a turntable, use a microwave baking sheet or a very large flat plate.)

▪

6 LAY four of the salmon strips close together on the paper to make a square. Working at right angles to the salmon, take one courgette slice and weave it under and over the strips of salmon. Repeat with two more courgette slices to make a neat square of plaited salmon and courgette.

▪

7 REPEAT with the remaining salmon and courgette to make four plaits, arranged side by side on the turntable or baking sheet.

▪

8 DOT with remaining butter and cover with a sheet of greaseproof paper, folding the edges together to completely enclose the salmon.

9 Cook on HIGH for about 5 minutes or until the fish is just cooked. Carefully remove from the cooker and arrange on four flat plates.

■

10 MEANWHILE, cook the sauce on HIGH for 2–3 minutes or until hot. Season to taste with salt and pepper, then spoon around the salmon and courgette plaits. Serve immediately.

■ *FISH WITH CORIANDER MASALA* ■

Definitely for those who love spicy food! If your fish is too large to fit in your microwave, follow the instructions in step 4 or, alternatively, remove the head and tail.

SERVES 2–3

1 medium onion, skinned and chopped
2 garlic cloves, skinned
1 green chilli, seeded (optional)
2.5 cm (1 inch) piece fresh root ginger, peeled
15 ml (1 level tbsp) coriander seeds
5 ml (1 level tsp) ground turmeric
5 ml (1 level tsp) fenugreek seeds
45 ml (3 tbsp) chopped fresh coriander
juice of 2 limes

30 ml (2 tbsp) vegetable oil
4 large tomatoes, finely chopped
15 ml (1 level tbsp) garam masala
salt
1 whole fish, such as whiting, codling or pollack, weighing about 700–900 g (1½–2 lb), scaled and cleaned
fresh coriander, to garnish

■

1 PUT the onion, garlic, chilli, ginger, coriander seeds, turmeric, fenugreek seeds, fresh coriander and lime juice in a blender or food processor and process until smooth.

■

2 PUT the oil in a large shallow dish (large enough to hold the fish) and cook on HIGH for 1 minute until hot. Add the spice paste and cook on HIGH for 5 minutes, or until the onion is softened, stirring occasionally.

■

3 ADD the tomatoes, garam masala and salt to taste and cook on HIGH for 3–4 minutes until the sauce is reduced and slightly thickened, stirring occasionally.

■

4 MEANWHILE, using a sharp knife, make deep cuts in a criss-cross pattern on each side of the fish. If the fish is too large for the microwave, push a long bamboo skewer through the tail and then into the body of the fish so that the tail is curved upwards.

■

5 LAY the fish in the dish containing the sauce and spoon the sauce over the fish to coat it. Cover and cook on HIGH for 10–15 minutes depending on the thickness of the fish, or until the fish is tender. Serve garnished with coriander.

· *HERRING AND VEGETABLE STIR FRY* ·

Silvery-skinned herrings are the perfect fish for stir frying as they will not break up during the quick cooking time.

SERVES 4

4 herrings, each weighing about 275 g (10 oz), cleaned and filleted
2 garlic cloves, skinned and crushed
45 ml (3 tbsp) sesame or vegetable oil
30 ml (2 tbsp) soy sauce

30 ml (2 tbsp) dry sherry
10 ml (2 level tsp) five-spice powder
175 g (6 oz) okra
1 red or yellow pepper, seeded
100 g (4 oz) mange-tout

■

1 CUT the herrings widthways into 2.5 cm (1 inch) strips and put into a bowl with the garlic, half the oil, the soy sauce, sherry and five-spice powder. Leave in a cool place to marinate for 30 minutes.

■

2 WHILE the fish is marinating, trim the okra and cut diagonally into 1 cm (½ inch) slices. Cut the pepper into strips about 0.5 cm (¼ inch) wide. Trim the mange-tout and cut in half if large.

■

3 PUT the remaining oil and the okra into a browning dish or a large bowl and cook on HIGH for 2–3 minutes or until the okra is slightly softened.

■

4 ADD the pepper and the mange-tout and cook on HIGH for 1–2 minutes, stirring once. Add the marinated fish and cook on HIGH for 3–4 minutes or until the fish is cooked, stirring occasionally but being careful not to break up the fish strips. Serve the stir fry immediately.

· *STUFFED HERRINGS* ·

The combination of fresh rosemary, dill, chives and sage is delicious. Herbs are now widely available in small boxes in supermarkets, but if you have difficulty in buying all four, substitute with others of your choice.

SERVES 4

4 herrings or mackerel, each weighing about 225 g (8 oz), cleaned and scaled
15 ml (1 tbsp) chopped fresh rosemary
15 ml (1 tbsp) chopped fresh dill
15 ml (1 tbsp) chopped fresh chives
15 ml (1 tbsp) chopped fresh sage
2 garlic cloves, skinned and chopped

50 g (2 oz) walnut halves, finely chopped
25 g (1 oz) fresh white breadcrumbs
salt and pepper
30 ml (2 tbsp) olive oil
30 ml (2 tbsp) lemon juice
walnut halves and fresh herbs, to garnish

1 REMOVE the head, tail and fins from the herrings, then cut completely along the underside. Open the fish out and lay cut side down on a board. Press lightly along the middle of the back to loosen the bone.

∎

2 TURN the fish over and ease out the backbone and as many small bones as possible. Wash and dry the fish.

∎

3 ARRANGE the fish, skin side down, in a large shallow dish, placing the wider end towards the outside. Sprinkle the fish with the herbs, garlic, walnuts and half the breadcrumbs. Season generously with pepper and a little salt. Carefully fold each fish in half.

∎

4 MIX the oil and lemon juice together and pour over the fish. Sprinkle with the remaining breadcrumbs. Cover and cook on HIGH for 8–10 minutes or until the fish is tender.

∎

5 SERVE with a little of the cooking liquid spooned over, garnished with a few walnut halves and herb sprigs.

▪ *TROUT WITH MUSHROOMS* ▪

Be careful when adding fish to a hot browning dish – if the fish is wet the fat in the dish will spit.

SERVES 2

2 trout, about 275 g (10 oz) each, cleaned
30 ml (2 tbsp) olive oil
15 g (½ oz) butter or margarine
175 g (6 oz) button mushrooms, thinly sliced

15 ml (1 tbsp) lemon juice
1 small garlic clove, skinned and crushed (optional)
45 ml (3 tbsp) double cream
salt and pepper
parsley sprigs, to garnish

∎

1 HEAT a browning dish on HIGH for 5–8 minutes or according to the manufacturer's instructions. Slash the fish twice on each side.

∎

2 ADD the oil to the browning dish, then quickly add the trout and cook on HIGH for 2 minutes or until browned on one side. Carefully turn the fish over and cook on HIGH for 2–3 minutes or until the fish is tender.

∎

3 TRANSFER the fish to a serving dish. Quickly add the remaining ingredients to the dish and cook on HIGH for 2–3 minutes until the mushrooms are just tender, stirring occasionally. Pour over the fish, garnish with parsley and serve immediately.

▪ *MACKEREL WITH CITRUS FRUIT* ▪

The combination of orange, lemon and lime juice makes a refreshing sauce which is perfect with oily fish such as mackerel.

Serves 4

1 medium orange
1 lemon
1 lime
4 mackerel, each weighing about 350 g
   (12 oz), cleaned

salt and pepper
chopped fresh parsley, to garnish

▪

1 Using a potato peeler or very sharp knife, peel the rind from the orange, lemon and lime. Remove and discard any white pith from the rind.

▪

2 Cut the rind into fine shreds and put into a large shallow dish. Squeeze the juice from the fruits into the dish with the rind.

▪

3 Cook on HIGH for 3–4 minutes or until the rind is slightly softened, stirring occasionally.

▪

4 Remove and discard the heads from the fish, then slash the skin twice on each side. Arrange in the dish, cover and cook on HIGH for about 10 minutes or until the fish is tender, rearranging the fish once during cooking. Season to taste with salt and pepper and serve immediately, garnished with chopped parsley.

▪ *LEAF-WRAPPED MULLET* ▪

Swiss chard makes a good wrapping for fish as the leaves are large and pliable and retain their bright green colour when cooked. It is a member of the beetroot family and is also known as seakale beet or silver beet.

Serves 4

4 red mullet, each weighing about
   275 g (10 oz), cleaned and scaled
3–4 garlic cloves, skinned
45 ml (3 tbsp) olive oil

30 ml (2 tbsp) white wine vinegar
salt and pepper
8 large Swiss chard or spinach leaves,
   trimmed

▪

1 Using a sharp knife, slash the mullet three times on each side. Roughly chop the garlic and sprinkle into the slashes. Whisk the oil and vinegar together and season to taste with salt and pepper.

▪

2 Put the fish into a shallow dish and pour over the oil and vinegar. Leave in a cool place for 30 minutes to marinate.

3 REMOVE the fish from the marinade and wrap each of them in two of the chard or spinach leaves. Return the wrapped fish to the dish containing the marinade.

■

4 COVER and cook on HIGH for 6–8 minutes or until the fish is tender, rearranging once and basting with the marinade during cooking.

■

5 SERVE the fish in their leaf parcels, with a little of the marinade spooned over.

■ *RED MULLET WITH RATATOUILLE* ■

This needs no accompaniment – except perhaps a bottle of wine!

SERVES 2

30 ml (2 tbsp) olive oil
1 medium onion, skinned and finely chopped
1 garlic clove, skinned and crushed
1 small aubergine, weighing about 225 g (8 oz)
1 large green pepper
226 g (8 oz) can tomatoes

15 ml (1 tbsp) tomato purée
1 bouquet garni
2 medium courgettes
salt and pepper
2 red mullet, each weighing about 175 g (6 oz), cleaned and scaled
chopped fresh parsley, to garnish

■

1 PUT half the oil into a large bowl with the onion and garlic. Cover and cook on HIGH for 2 minutes until the onion is slightly softened.

■

2 MEANWHILE, trim the aubergine and cut into 0.5 cm (¼ inch) slices. Cut the slices in half if they are large. Remove the seeds from the pepper, then cut the pepper into 0.5 cm (¼ inch) slices.

■

3 ADD the aubergine, pepper, tomatoes and their juice, tomato purée and bouquet garni to the onion. Re-cover and cook on HIGH for 8–10 minutes until the vegetables are cooked, stirring occasionally.

■

4 CUT the courgettes into 0.5 cm (¼ inch) slices and stir into the ratatouille. Season generously with salt and pepper.

■

5 SLASH the fish twice on each side and place in a large shallow dish. Pour over the remaining olive oil. Stand the dish containing the fish on top of the bowl containing the ratatouille. Cover the fish and cook on HIGH for 5–6 minutes until the fish is cooked.

■

6 To serve, divide the ratatouille between two plates and arrange a fish on top of each. Sprinkle generously with chopped parsley.

· GREY MULLET WITH POMEGRANATES ·

Pomegranates always look so tempting when displayed in greengrocers or market stalls. They are rarely used in cooking, but here they are made into a delicious, gleaming red sauce which contrasts perfectly with the creamy white mullet.

SERVES 4–6

4 ripe pomegranates
1 cinnamon stick
10 ml (2 level tsp) caster sugar
5 ml (1 tsp) red wine vinegar

1 grey mullet, weighing about 1.4 kg
  (3 lb), scaled and cleaned
a few bay leaves
25 g (1 oz) butter or margarine

■

1 PLACE a sieve over a medium bowl. Cut the pomegranates in half and scoop out the seeds into the sieve. Press the seeds with a wooden spoon to extract the juice.

■

2 ADD the cinnamon, sugar and vinegar to the pomegranate juice and cook on HIGH for 3–4 minutes until just boiling.

■

3 WHILE the sauce is cooking, separate about 45 ml (3 tbsp) of the seeds remaining in the sieve from the course white membrane. Discard the remaining seeds and membrane.

■

4 ADD the seeds to the sauce and set aside while cooking the fish.

■

5 REMOVE and discard the head from the fish, then cut a criss cross pattern on each side of the fish. Put the bay leaves into the cavity.

■

6 SMEAR a large piece of greaseproof paper with the butter or margarine. Wrap the fish in the paper and then in a second piece to make a neat parcel.

■

7 COOK on HIGH for 9–12 minutes or until the fish is tender, turning the fish once during cooking.

■

8 COOK the sauce on HIGH for 2 minutes or until hot, then discard the cinnamon stick.

■

9 UNWRAP the fish and transfer to a serving platter, then pour over the sauce. Serve immediately.

Mediterranean Fish Stew (page 82)

· MACARONI AND SARDINE AU GRATIN ·

This unusual gratin is a good way to make use of sardines.

Serves 4–6

1 small fennel bulb, trimmed and
  chopped
1 medium onion, skinned and chopped
397 g (14 oz) can tomatoes
10 ml (2 tsp) tomato purée
60 ml (4 tbsp) dry white wine, fish or
  vegetable stock (see pages 125 and
  123)
450 g (1 lb) sardines, cleaned and scaled
100 g (4 oz) sultanas

75 g (3 oz) pine nuts
275 g (10 oz) short cut macaroni
salt and pepper
30 ml (2 tbsp) freshly grated Parmesan
  cheese
50 g (2 oz) fresh breadcrumbs
chopped fresh fennel or parsley, to
  garnish

■

1 PUT the fennel and the onion into a large gratin dish with the tomatoes, tomato purée and wine or stock. Cover and cook on HIGH for 10–12 minutes or until the vegetables are softened.

■

2 MEANWHILE, remove the heads from the sardines, then cut completely along the belly. Open the fish out flat and lay cut side down on a chopping board. Press firmly along the middle of the back with your fingers to loosen the backbone. Turn the fish over and remove the backbone.

■

3 CUT the sardines in half, or into quarters, if large. Stir into the tomato sauce with half the sultanas and half the pine nuts. Re-cover and cook on HIGH for 2–3 minutes or until the fish is cooked, stirring once.

■

4 PUT the macaroni into a large bowl and pour over enough boiling water to cover the pasta by about 2.5 cm (1 inch). Cover and cook on HIGH for 7–10 minutes until tender.

■

5 DRAIN the macaroni and mix into the tomato sauce. Season to taste with salt and pepper and lightly toss together so that all of the pasta is coated in the sauce. Level the surface.

■

6 MIX the cheese and the breadcrumbs together and sprinkle on top of the pasta. Brown under a hot grill, then sprinkle with the remaining pine nuts and sultanas. Garnish with chopped fennel or parsley and serve hot with a salad.

Red Snapper and Root Vegetables with Spicy Oil (page 84)

· *MEDITERRANEAN FISH STEW* ·

This makes very generous servings for six people with hearty appetites!

Serves 6

25 g (1 oz) butter or margarine
2 celery sticks, trimmed and chopped
3 carrots, sliced
225 g (8 oz) baby onions, skinned
2 strips of lemon rind
2 garlic cloves, skinned and crushed
1 bouquet garni
pinch of saffron
397 g (14 oz) can tomatoes
150 ml (¼ pint) fish or vegetable stock
  (see pages 125 and 123)
150 ml (¼ pint) dry red wine

6 small red mullet, each weighing
  about 175 g (6 oz), cleaned and
  scaled
6 conger eel steaks, each weighing
  about 150 g (5 oz)
225 g (8 oz) mussels, cleaned (see
  page 12)
salt and pepper
chopped fresh parsley, chopped garlic
  and grated lemon rind, to garnish
  (optional)

■

1 Put the butter, celery, carrots, onions, lemon rind, garlic, bouquet garni, saffron, tomatoes with their juice, fish or vegetable stock and wine into a large bowl. Cover and cook on HIGH for 10–12 minutes or until the vegetables are almost tender, stirring occasionally.

■

2 Meanwhile, remove and discard the heads from the mullet.

■

3 Add the eel steaks to the stew and push down into the sauce. Lay the mullet on top. Cover and cook for 6–8 minutes or until the fish is tender, stirring once.

■

4 Add the mussels, re-cover and cook on HIGH for 3 minutes or until the mussels are open. Discard any which do not open. Season generously with salt and pepper.

■

5 To serve, divide the stew between six soup bowls, allowing one mullet and one eel steak per portion. Sprinkle with parsley, garlic and lemon rind, if wished, and serve immediately with French bread.

· *FISH MOUSSAKA* ·

Moussaka is much quicker to make in the microwave, especially if you cook the aubergines slightly as in step 1. Follow this method if converting other conventional recipes which include layers of aubergine.

Serves 4–6

2 aubergines, each weighing about
   225 g (8 oz)
15 ml (1 tbsp) vegetable oil
1 medium onion, skinned and finely
   chopped
1 garlic clove, skinned and crushed
5 ml (1 level tsp) ground cinnamon
5 ml (1 level tsp) dried oregano
397 g (14 oz) can tomatoes

15 ml (1 tbsp) tomato purée
700 g (1½ lb) oily fish fillets, such as
   mackerel, herring or pilchard,
   skinned
salt and pepper
2 eggs, beaten
300ml (½ pint) natural yogurt
grated nutmeg
15 g (½ oz) grated Parmesan cheese

1 PRICK the aubergines all over with a fork and rub with a little of the oil. Place on a piece of absorbent kitchen paper and cook on HIGH for 3–4 minutes or until slightly softened. Do not overcook or the aubergines will be difficult to slice. Leave to cool while cooking the filling.

2 To make the filling, put the onion, garlic, half the cinnamon, the oregano, tomatoes and their juice, tomato purée and remaining oil in a medium bowl. Cook on HIGH for 7–8 minutes, stirring two or three times until the onion is soft and the sauce is slightly reduced.

3 MEANWHILE, cut the fish into small pieces.

4 WHEN the tomato sauce is cooked, add the fish and cook on HIGH for 4–5 minutes until the fish flakes easily. Season to taste with salt and pepper.

5 SPOON half the fish and tomato sauce into a flameproof dish. Using a serrated knife, thinly slice the aubergines and arrange half on top of the sauce. Repeat the layers once, ending with a layer of aubergine.

6 To make the topping, beat the eggs and remaining cinnamon into the yogurt. Season generously with nutmeg and salt and pepper. Spoon evenly on top of the aubergines.

7 COOK on MEDIUM for 12–14 minutes until the topping is set around the edge but still slightly liquid in the centre. Sprinkle with the Parmesan cheese and brown under a preheated grill.

• RED SNAPPER AND ROOT VEGETABLES WITH SPICY OIL •

This unusual combination makes a filling meal and needs no other accompaniment.

SERVES 4

1 green chilli
5 ml (1 level tsp) ground aniseed
2 allspice berries
60 ml (4 tbsp) vegetable oil
225 g (8 oz) celeriac
225 g (8 oz) parsnips

225 g (8 oz) carrots
4 red snapper or red mullet, each
   weighing about 275 g (10 oz),
   cleaned and scaled
salt and pepper
chopped fresh parsley, to garnish

1 REMOVE the seeds from the chilli and discard. Finely chop the chilli and put into a small bowl with the aniseed. Crush the allspice berries and add with the oil. Cook on HIGH for 1–2 minutes or until hot, then leave to infuse while cooking the vegetables.

2 PEEL the celeriac, parsnips and carrots. Cut the celeriac and parsnips into neat strips about 7.5 cm (3 inches) long and 1 cm (½ inch) wide. Cut the carrots into diagonal slices about 1 cm (½ inch) thick. Put all of the vegetables in a medium bowl with 45 ml (3 tbsp) water. Cover and cook on HIGH for 5–6 minutes or until slightly softened, stirring once.

3 USING a sharp knife, slash the fish twice on each side and arrange in a single layer in a large dish. Brush with a little of the spicy oil, cover and put in the cooker on top of the bowl containing the vegetables. Cook on HIGH for 7–8 minutes or until the fish is tender, rearranging the fish once during cooking.

4 COOK the remaining oil on HIGH for 1 minute or until hot, then drain the vegetables and toss in half the hot oil. Season to taste with salt and pepper.

5 ARRANGE the vegetables on a serving platter with the fish. Spoon the remaining hot oil over the fish, garnish with parsley and serve immediately.

· MINT MARINATED TUNA FISH ·

Tuna is a very dense fish and takes longer to cook than white fish – the cooking time depends on the thickness, if your steaks are thicker than 2.5 cm (1 inch) you may need to increase the cooking time given here by 1–2 minutes. Serve with new potatoes in their skins.

SERVES 4

1 garlic clove, skinned and crushed
60 ml (4 tbsp) chopped fresh mint
30 ml (2 tbsp) olive oil
salt and pepper
4 tuna steaks, each weighing about
    225 g (8 oz)

30 ml (2 tbsp) lemon juice
225 g (8 oz) cherry tomatoes
45 ml (3 tbsp) dry white wine
fresh mint, to garnish

■

1 IN a small bowl, mix the garlic, half the mint, a little of the olive oil and salt and pepper to taste, to a smooth paste. Rub the paste all over the tuna steaks. Arrange them in a single layer in a shallow dish.

■

2 BLEND the remaining oil and lemon juice together and pour over the fish. Cover and leave in a cool place to marinate for 2–3 hours or overnight, turning the fish over once.

■

3 To cook the tuna, cover and cook on HIGH for 12–15 minutes or until the fish flakes easily.

■

4 WHILE the fish is cooking, prick each tomato several times with a skewer or the point of a sharp knife to prevent it from bursting during cooking.

■

5 REMOVE the tuna from the cooking liquid and arrange on four serving plates. Add the remaining mint and the white wine and cherry tomatoes to the liquid and cook on HIGH for 2 minutes or until bubbling and the tomatoes are just warm. Season to taste with salt and pepper.

■

6 To serve, arrange a few tomatoes on each plate and spoon the sauce over the fish. Garnish with fresh mint and serve immediately with new potatoes in their skins.

· SEA BASS COOKED WITH A SPICE PASTE ·

A mixture of spices, almonds and coconut makes a delicious coating for the magnificent sea bass.

SERVES 6

1 green chilli, seeded and chopped
2 garlic cloves, skinned and crushed
30 ml (2 level tbsp) desiccated coconut
45 ml (3 level tbsp) ground almonds
45 ml (3 tbsp) chopped fresh coriander
2.5 cm (1 inch) piece fresh root ginger, peeled and grated
10 ml (2 level tsp) ground cumin
5 ml (1 level tsp) ground cardamom

5 ml (1 level tsp) ground mixed spice
finely grated rind and juice of 1 lime
salt and pepper
1 sea bass, weighing about 1.5 kg (3½ lb), cleaned and scaled
30 ml (2 tbsp) olive oil
lime slices and fresh coriander, to garnish

1 PUT the chilli, garlic, coconut, almonds, coriander, ginger, cumin, cardamom, mixed spice and lime rind and juice in a blender or food processor with 150 ml (¼ pint) water and purée until smooth. Season to taste with salt and pepper.

2 USING a sharp knife, remove and discard the head and tail from the fish, then make four or five deep cuts on each side of the fish. Spread the spice paste into the cuts and all over the fish.

3 PUT the fish in a shallow dish and pour over the oil. Cover and cook on HIGH for about 13–15 minutes or until the fish is tender and looks opaque. Leave to stand for 5 minutes.

4 SERVE garnished with lime slices and fresh coriander.

· WHOLE FISH COOKED IN A BAMBOO LEAF PARCEL ·

Bamboo leaves are available from Chinese stores. They are very cheap and make an attractive wrapping for whole fish. If you cannot find them, wrap the fish in a double layer of greaseproof paper instead.

SERVES 2–3

1 whole fish such as bass, bream, red snapper or grey mullet, weighing about 700 g (1½ lb), scaled and cleaned
2.5 cm (1 inch) piece fresh root ginger, peeled

2 garlic cloves, skinned
2 spring onions, trimmed
6 bamboo leaves, washed
5 ml (1 level tsp) five-spice powder
15 ml (1 tbsp) vegetable oil
15 ml (1 tbsp) soy sauce

1 USING a sharp knife, make several slashes on each side of the fish.

■

2 THINLY slice the ginger and the garlic. Cut the spring onions into very thin strips.

■

3 LAY three bamboo leaves on a flat surface, overlapping them slightly, then lay the fish on top. Sprinkle with the ginger, garlic, spring onions and five-spice powder. Mix the vegetable oil and soy sauce together and spoon over the fish.

■

4 OVERLAP the remaining bamboo leaves on top of the fish. Wrap fine string around the fish and leaves so that the fish is completely enclosed in a neat parcel.

■

5 COOK on HIGH for 8–10 minutes or until the fish is cooked, turning the fish over once during cooking. (Pull the leaves slightly apart to check the fish.)

■

6 SERVE the fish in its bamboo leaf parcel.

■ *SWORDFISH POACHED IN A BASIL VINAIGRETTE* ■

Swordfish is now becoming more widely available. It has a firm almost meat-like texture and lots of flavour.

SERVES 2

45 ml (3 tbsp) olive oil
30 ml (2 tbsp) lemon juice
30 ml (2 tbsp) chopped fresh basil
salt and pepper

2 swordfish or tuna fish steaks, each weighing about 275 g (10 oz)
basil leaves, to garnish

■

1 WHISK the oil, lemon juice and basil together and season generously with salt and pepper.

■

2 ARRANGE the fish in a single layer in a large shallow dish and pour over the vinaigrette. Cover and cook on HIGH for 5–8 minutes or until the fish is tender, basting occasionally during cooking. The cooking time will depend on the thickness of the fish.

■

3 TO serve, transfer the fish to two serving plates and spoon over the vinaigrette. Garnish with basil and serve immediately.

· CONGER EEL STEW ·

Conger eel is now sold in cutlets in some fishmongers. It is a firm meaty fish that keeps its shape during cooking, making it ideal for stews.

SERVES 4

450 g (1 lb) very ripe tomatoes, skinned
15 ml (1 tbsp) olive oil
15 ml (1 tbsp) tomato purée
2 garlic cloves, skinned and crushed
2.5 ml (½ level tsp) ground nutmeg
150 ml (¼ pint) dry white wine

1 green pepper, seeded and chopped
45 ml (3 tbsp) chopped fresh parsley
salt and pepper
4 conger eel cutlets, each weighing
    about 225 g (8 oz)
4 slices of French bread

·

1 ROUGHLY chop the tomatoes and put into a bowl with the oil, tomato purée, garlic, nutmeg and wine. Cook on HIGH for 8–10 minutes until the tomatoes are soft and the sauce is slightly reduced, stirring occasionally.

·

2 ADD the green pepper, cover and cook on HIGH for 2 minutes until the pepper is softened. Stir in half the parsley and season to taste with salt and pepper.

·

3 SPOON half the sauce into a large serving dish and arrange the eel on top. Spoon over the remaining sauce. Cover and cook on HIGH for 6–7 minutes until the fish is tender.

·

4 WHILE the fish is cooking, toast the French bread on both sides.

·

5 To serve, sprinkle the toasted bread with the remaining parsley and arrange on top of the stew. Serve immediately.

· JOHN DORY WITH CELERIAC AND POTATOES ·

John Dory has a very large head which accounts for almost two thirds of its total weight. Although it is in season throughout the year, it is rarely seen for sale so it is worth buying when it does appear. This makes a delicious meal that needs no other accompaniment.

SERVES 2

350 g (12 oz) potatoes
350 g (12 oz) celeriac
juice of ½ a lemon
45 ml (3 tbsp) double cream
30 ml (2 tbsp) chopped fresh parsley

salt and pepper
4 John Dory, sole or flounder fillets,
    each weighing about 75 g (3 oz),
    skinned
15 g (½ oz) butter or margarine

1 PEEL the potatoes and the celeriac and cut into strips about 0.5 cm (¼ inch) thick and 4 cm (1½ inches) long. Put into a small shallow dish and toss with the lemon juice. Cover and cook on HIGH for 6–8 minutes until the vegetables are almost tender.

■

2 CAREFULLY mix the cream, half the parsley and salt and pepper into the vegetables. Cut each fish fillet in half, then lay them on top of the vegetables. Dot with the butter or margarine and sprinkle with the remaining parsley.

■

3 COVER and cook on HIGH for 3–4 minutes until the fish is tender. Serve immediately.

■ CRAB WITH WATER CHESTNUTS AND BLACK BEAN SAUCE ■

Fermented black beans, which are whole soya beans preserved in ginger and salt, are used to make a rich sauce.

SERVES 4

½ a cucumber
30 ml (2 tbsp) fermented black beans
2 garlic cloves, skinned and thinly sliced
30 ml (2 tbsp) dry sherry
15 ml (1 tbsp) soy sauce
5 ml (1 level tsp) sugar
finely grated rind and juice of 1 lemon

450 g (1 lb) cooked crab meat (see page 13)
228 g (8 oz) can water chestnuts, drained and sliced
4 spring onions, trimmed
10 ml (2 level tsp) cornflour
spring onion tassels, to garnish

■

1 CUT the cucumber into very thin slices and arrange around the edge of a serving platter.

■

2 PUT the black beans and 30 ml (2 tbsp) water in a medium bowl and mash together. Add the garlic, sherry, soy sauce, sugar and the lemon rind and juice and mix thoroughly together.

■

3 ADD the crab meat and the water chestnuts, cover and cook on HIGH for 3–4 minutes until hot, stirring once. Meanwhile, cut the spring onions into 2.5 cm (1 inch) lengths. Blend the cornflour to a smooth paste with a little water.

■

5 STIR the spring onions and cornflour into the crab mixture and cook on HIGH for 1–2 minutes until slightly thickened, stirring once. Spoon on to the platter with the sliced cucumber, garnish with the spring onion tassels and serve immediately with rice or noodles.

· SWEET AND SOUR GOLDEN CARP ·

Carp is one of the most attractive fish to look at, but one of the most difficult to eat because it is very bony.

SERVES 2–3

1 large, almost ripe, mango
30 ml (2 tbsp) orange juice
30 ml (2 tbsp) white wine vinegar
1 golden carp, weighing about
    700–900 g (1½–2 lb), scaled and
    cleaned
15 ml (1 tbsp) clear honey

30 ml (2 tbsp) soy sauce
2.5 ml (½ level tsp) ground ginger
5 ml (1 level tsp) paprika
30 ml (2 level tbsp) dark soft brown
    sugar
watercress or fresh herbs, to garnish

■

1 Cut two thick slices from the mango, one each side of the central stone. Cut one of the slices lengthways into three thick slices, peel and reserve. Peel and roughly chop the remaining mango.

■

2 Using a teaspoon, scrape the flesh from the mango stone and put into a blender or food processor with chopped mango, orange juice, and vinegar and purée until smooth.

■

3 Cut three deep slashes on each side of the carp. Push a slice of mango into each slash on one side. If the fish is too large for the microwave, push a long bamboo skewer through the tail and then into the body of the fish so that the tail is curved upwards. Alternatively remove the head and tail.

■

4 Mix the honey, soy sauce, ginger and paprika together and spread all over the uppermost side of the fish. Sprinkle with the sugar.

■

5 Place the fish in a large shallow dish and cook on HIGH for 10–15 minutes, depending on the thickness of the fish.

■

6 Pour the puréed mango mixture into a small bowl and cook on HIGH for 2–3 minutes or until hot. Serve the fish whole with the sauce handed separately, garnished with watercress or fresh herbs.

· *SPAGHETTI NEST WITH SHELLFISH* ·

Don't forget to put some empty bowls on the table to put the discarded shells in. This is not a dish to serve to those who don't like getting their fingers messy!

SERVES 4

900 g (2 lb) mixed shellfish, such as fresh mussels, venus clams, raw prawns, cleaned (see pages 12 and 13)
150 ml (¼ pint) dry white wine
450 g (1 lb) spaghetti
30 ml (2 tbsp) vegetable oil

1–2 garlic cloves, skinned and crushed
2.5–5 ml (½–1 level tsp) cayenne pepper (optional)
30 ml (2 tbsp) roughly chopped fresh parsley
salt and black pepper

■

1 PUT the shellfish and the wine into a large bowl. Cover and cook on HIGH for about 4–7 minutes or until all of the mussels and clams have opened, removing the mussels and clams on the top as they open and shaking the bowl occasionally. Discard any which do not open. Drain, reserving the cooking liquid.

■

2 PUT the spaghetti into a large bowl and pour over enough boiling water to cover the pasta by about 2.5 cm (1 inch). Cover and cook on HIGH for 7–10 minutes or until almost tender. Leave to stand while finishing the sauce. Do not drain.

■

3 ADD the oil, garlic and cayenne pepper to the reserved cooking liquid and cook on HIGH for 4 minutes until slightly reduced. Return the shellfish to the bowl with the parsley and cook on HIGH for 2 minutes until hot, stirring once.

■

4 USING a slotted spoon, remove the shellfish and arrange in the centre of four plates. Drain the pasta and toss in the sauce remaining in the bowl. Arrange around the shellfish to make a 'nest' on each plate. Season generously with black pepper and a little salt. Serve immediately.

· COLD FISH DISHES ·

What could be more delicious in the summer than a lightly chilled dish of melt-in-the-mouth fish, cooked to perfection in the microwave? This chapter contains a wide selection of such dishes. As they all require cooling before serving they are perfect to cook in advance and then serve as a starter or as part of a buffet. The fish salads make a delicious main meal for lunch or supper.

As with all chilled, cooked foods, it is important to cool the hot fish quickly then cover and chill it in the refrigerator until just before serving. Remove from the fridge about 30 minutes before serving for maximum flavour.

· *PLAICE WITH ORANGE AND YOGURT MAYONNAISE* ·

This dish can be made equally well with other flat fish fillets.

SERVES 4

8 plaice fillets, each weighing about 75 g (3 oz)
30 ml (2 tbsp) fish or vegetable stock (see pages 125 and 123) or milk
45 ml (3 tbsp) mayonnaise (see page 126)

finely grated rind and juice of ½ a medium orange
45 ml (3 tbsp) natural yogurt
orange slices, to garnish

·

1 CUT each plaice fillet into two pieces and arrange in a single layer in a shallow dish. Pour over the stock or milk, cover and cook on HIGH for 3–4 minutes or until tender. Leave to cool, covered.

·

2 To make the orange and yogurt mayonnaise, mix the mayonnaise with the orange rind and juice and the yogurt. Chill until ready to serve.

·

3 To serve, drain the fish and arrange on a serving platter. Coat in the mayonnaise, garnish with orange slices and serve immediately.

• TARAMASALATA TERRINE WITH SEAWEED •

This delicious terrine takes very little effort to make and is impressive enough for a buffet or dinner party.

SERVES 8

40 g (1½ oz) butter or margarine
45 ml (3 level tbsp) plain flour
300 ml (½ pint) milk
450 g (1 lb) white fish fillets, such as
    cod, haddock, coley, whiting or
    monkfish, skinned
300 ml (½ pint) double cream
3 eggs
5 ml (1 tsp) anchovy essence

30 ml (2 tbsp) chopped mixed herbs,
    such as chervil, chives, tarragon, dill
    and parsley
salt and pepper
225 g (8 oz) good quality taramasalata
10 ml (2 tsp) tomato purée
2 sheets of nori each measuring about
    20.5×18 cm (8×7 inches)

■

1 GREASE a 1.7 litre (3 pint) loaf dish and line the base with greaseproof paper. Grease the paper.

■

2 PUT the butter or margarine, flour and milk into a large bowl and cook on HIGH for 3–4 minutes until boiling and very thick, whisking frequently.

■

3 MEANWHILE, roughly chop the fish and put into a blender or food processor with the cream and eggs.

■

4 WHEN the sauce is cooked, pour into the blender or food processor and purée the mixture until smooth. Transfer half the mixture to a bowl and mix with the anchovy essence and the herbs. Season with salt and pepper.

■

5 ADD the taramasalata and tomato purée to the remaining mixture and process until well mixed. Season to taste with salt and pepper.

■

6 SPOON half of the taramasalata mixture into the base of the loaf dish and level the surface. Fold one sheet of nori in half, then lay on top.

■

7 SPOON the white fish mixture on top of the nori and level the surface. Fold the second sheet of nori in half and place on top. Spoon the remaining taramasalata mixture on top and level the surface.

■

8 COVER with a piece of greaseproof paper, stand the dish on a roasting rack and cook on MEDIUM for about 20 minutes or until the terrine feels firm to the touch and is slightly risen in the centre. Leave to cool in the dish. Unmould the terrine on to a serving plate. Serve cut into slices.

▪ *TROUT WITH SESAME CREAM* ▪

This unusual way of serving cold poached trout makes a delicious main course dish served with a salad or rice pilaff.

SERVES 2–4

2 trout, total weight about 275 g
  (10 oz)
15 ml (1 tbsp) vegetable oil
60 ml (4 tbsp) tahini (sesame seed
  paste)
30 ml (2 tbsp) lemon juice
150 ml (¼ pint) soured cream

1 garlic clove, skinned and crushed
  (optional)
30 ml (2 tbsp) finely chopped fresh
  parsley
salt and pepper
tarragon or flat leaf parsley and black
  olives, to garnish

▪

1 BRUSH the trout with the oil and arrange in a single layer in a shallow dish. Cover and cook on HIGH for 5–7 minutes or until tender. Carefully peel off the skin, leaving the head and tail intact. Leave to cool.

▪

2 To make the sauce, put the tahini, lemon juice, soured cream, garlic, if using, and parsley into a bowl and mix together. Season to taste with salt and pepper.

▪

3 CAREFULLY transfer the fish to two plates. Coat in some of the sauce, leaving the head and tail exposed. Garnish with tarragon or parsley leaves and olives. Serve with the remaining sauce and a salad or rice pilaff.

▪ *GEFILLTE FISH* ▪

Gefillte fish is a traditional Jewish recipe. It was originally a fish stuffing made from finely chopped fish used to stuff large freshwater fish such as bream or carp. Today freshwater or seafish is made into balls, poached in fish stock and served cold.

SERVES 4

450 ml (¾ pint) fish or vegetable stock
  (see pages 125 and 123)
450 g (1 lb) bream, carp, hake or
  haddock fillets, skinned
225 g (½ lb) cod fillet, skinned
1 medium onion, skinned and chopped
30 ml (2 tbsp) vegetable oil

1 egg, beaten
30 ml (2 level tbsp) medium matzo
  meal
30 ml (2 level tbsp) ground almonds
salt and pepper
lemon wedges and fresh parsley, to
  garnish

▪

1 PUT the stock into a large shallow dish and cook on HIGH for about 15 minutes or until reduced by half.

▪

2 MEANWHILE, make the fish balls. Cut the fish into chunks, put into a blender or food processor and chop roughly. Add the onion and oil and continue to process until the fish is very finely chopped.

3 TRANSFER the mixture to a bowl and add the egg, matzo meal, almonds and season to taste with salt and pepper. Mix together thoroughly, the mixture should be stiff enough to shape into balls. If it is too soft, add a little more matzo meal.

■

4 WITH wetted hands, shape the mixture into twelve balls. Arrange the balls in the stock, placing them around the edge of the dish. Cover and cook on MEDIUM for 8–10 minutes or until firm to the touch.

■

5 LIFT the balls out of the stock and arrange on a serving platter. Cover and leave until cold. Serve at room temperature, garnished with lemon wedges and parsley or serve with Tomato Sauce (see page 123).

■ *BRILL WITH GREEN SAUCE* ■

Although brill are in season all the year round, they are not widely available. If you see some for sale do buy them and try this recipe.

SERVES 4–6

8 brill, plaice or sole fillets, each
  weighing about 75 g (3 oz), skinned
30 ml (2 tbsp) fish or vegetable stock
  (see pages 125 and 123) or milk
225 g (8 oz) broccoli
100 g (4 oz) French beans
2 medium courgettes

45 ml (3 tbsp) mayonnaise (see page
  126)
45 ml (3 tbsp) natural yogurt
15 ml (1 tbsp) lemon juice
45 ml (3 tbsp) chopped fresh herbs
salt and pepper
fresh herbs, to garnish

■

1 CUT each fillet into two pieces and arrange around the edge of a shallow dish. Pour over the stock or milk, cover and cook on HIGH for 3–4 minutes until tender. Leave to cool, covered.

■

2 TRIM the broccoli and cut into tiny florets. Top and tail beans and cut into 5 cm (2 inch) pieces. Slice courgettes into 0.5 cm (¼ inch) slices.

■

3 PUT the vegetables into a bowl with 15 ml (1 tbsp) water. Cover and cook on HIGH for 2–3 minutes until softened but still crisp. Drain, rinse with cold water and leave to cool.

■

4 To make the sauce, put the mayonnaise, yogurt, lemon juice and herbs into a bowl and beat together. Season to taste with salt and pepper. Chill until ready to serve.

■

5 To serve, arrange the fish and vegetables on a plate, spoon over a little of the green sauce and serve immediately, garnished with fresh herbs and with the remaining sauce handed separately.

▪ *MIXED FISH SALAD* ▪

A delicious and colourful mixture of fish, seafood and vegetables.

SERVES 6

450 g (1 lb) fresh mussels or venus
  clams in the shell, cleaned (see
  page 12)
150 ml (¼ pint) dry white wine
450 g (1 lb) monkfish, skinned
450 g (1 lb) squid, cleaned (see
  page 11)
75 g (3 oz) mange tout
1 red pepper

2 medium carrots
175 g (6 oz) cooked peeled prawns or
  350 g (12 oz) prawns in the shell
150 ml (¼ pint) olive oil
45 ml (3 tbsp) white wine vinegar
1–2 garlic cloves, skinned and crushed
salt and pepper
45 ml (3 tbsp) chopped fresh parsley
50 g (2 oz) black olives

▪

1 PUT the mussels or clams into a large bowl with half of the wine. Cover and cook on HIGH for 3–5 minutes or until all of the mussels or clams have opened, removing the ones on the top as they open and shaking the bowl occasionally. Discard any which do not open.

▪

2 CUT the monkfish into 2.5 cm (1 inch) chunks and put into a large shallow dish with a flat bottom. Slice the squid into small rings and the tentacles into 2.5 cm (1 inch) pieces. Put into the dish with the monkfish and pour over the remaining wine.

▪

3 COVER and cook on HIGH for 4–5 minutes until the monkfish and squid look opaque, stirring once.

▪

4 USING a slotted spoon, remove the monkfish and squid from the wine and transfer to a large salad bowl. Strain the wine from the mussels into the dish with the wine from the monkfish and squid.

▪

5 COOK the wine on HIGH for 8–10 minutes until boiling and reduced by half. Leave to cool.

▪

6 REMOVE the mussels or clams from their shells, if liked, and mix with the other fish. Leave to cool.

▪

7 TRIM the mange tout and cut in half if large. Put into a bowl with 15 ml (1 tbsp) water, cover and cook on HIGH for 1 minute. Rinse in cold water, drain and mix with the fish.

▪

8 CORE and seed the pepper and scrub the carrots, then cut them both into neat thin strips. Mix with the fish. Stir in the prawns.

Opposite: *Trout with Sesame Cream (page 94)*
Overleaf: *Brill with Green Sauce (page 95)*

9 WHISK the oil, vinegar, garlic, salt and pepper to taste and the parsley into the reduced wine and pour over the salad. Add the olives, then carefully mix everything together. Chill for at least 2 hours before serving to let the flavours develop.

▪ *HOT, SWEET AND SOUR FISH AND FLAGEOLET SALAD* ▪

Use two cans of flageolet beans instead of dried ones in this salad, if you prefer. Serve with a contrasting salad of tomato and cucumber and granary bread.

SERVES 4

175 g (6 oz) flageolet beans, soaked overnight
2 mackerel, each weighing about 350 g (12 oz), cleaned
1 large orange
30 ml (2 tbsp) red wine vinegar
30 ml (2 tbsp) soy sauce
30 ml (2 tbsp) tomato purée
15 ml (1 tbsp) clear honey

5 ml (1 level tsp) mild paprika
5 ml (1 level tsp) chilli powder
2.5 cm (1 inch) piece fresh root ginger, peeled and grated
1 garlic clove, skinned and crushed
salt and pepper
½ an iceberg lettuce
handful of coriander leaves

▪

1 DRAIN the beans, then put into a large bowl and cover with enough water to come about 2.5 cm (1 inch) above the level of the beans. Cover and cook on HIGH for 40–50 minutes or until tender, stirring occasionally. Leave to stand.

▪

2 WHILE the beans are standing, remove the heads and tails from the mackerel, then put the fish into a large shallow dish with the juice from half of the orange. Cover and cook on HIGH for 5–6 minutes or until the fish flakes easily.

▪

3 LEAVE the fish until cool enough to handle, then remove the skin and bones and cut the flesh into large chunks. Leave to cool.

▪

4 To make the dressing, mix the remaining orange juice, vinegar, soy sauce, tomato purée, honey, paprika, chilli powder, ginger and garlic together. Season to taste with salt and pepper.

▪

5 DRAIN the beans and mix with the dressing. Leave to cool.

▪

6 WHEN the beans are cool, cut the lettuce into bite-sized chunks and mix into the beans with the fish. Toss carefully together, sprinkle with the coriander leaves, and serve immediately.

▪ *TURBAN OF SALMON AND SOLE WITH TARRAGON SAUCE* ▪

This looks and tastes delicious, but is an expensive dish. To make a cheaper version, instead of salmon use a firm white fish, such as cod or haddock, and just enough tomato purée to colour it pink.

SERVES 6–8

350 g (12 oz) fresh salmon
2 egg whites
150 ml (¼ pint) double cream
300 ml (½ pint) Greek strained yogurt
salt and pepper

50 g (2 oz) cooked peeled prawns
8 lemon sole fillets, skinned
150 ml (¼ pint) dry white wine
15 ml (1 tbsp) chopped fresh tarragon
fresh tarragon leaves, to garnish

▪

1 GREASE a 1.1 litre (2 pint) ring mould.

▪

2 REMOVE and discard the skin and bones from the salmon. Roughly chop the flesh, then purée in a blender or food processor until smooth.

▪

3 WITH the machine still running, gradually add the egg whites, cream and half the yogurt. Season to taste with salt and pepper, then stir in the prawns. Chill for about 30 minutes until firm.

▪

4 MEANWHILE, lay the sole fillets on a chopping board and flatten slightly with the flat edge of a large knife. Very lightly slash the skin side of each fillet two or three times being careful not to cut the flesh.

▪

5 ARRANGE the fillets in the greased mould, skin side upwards, like the spokes of a wheel, spacing them equally around the mould and letting the ends of the fillets hang over the inside and outside edges.

▪

6 SPOON the chilled salmon mixture into the lined mould and level the surface. Fold the ends of the sole fillets over the salmon mixture.

▪

7 COVER with greaseproof paper and cook on MEDIUM for 7–8 minutes until firm to the touch. Leave to stand for 10 minutes.

▪

8 UNCOVER and place a wire rack over the top of the mould. Invert the rack and mould on to a baking tray or shallow dish to catch the liquid that will run out of the mould. (Reserve the liquid for the sauce.) Leave to drain for about 5 minutes, then turn over again so that the turban is still in the mould and the rack is on top.

▪

9 REMOVE the rack, then unmould the turban on to a serving plate. Leave to cool.

10 To make the sauce, put the wine into a bowl and cook on HIGH for 6–7 minutes until reduced by half. Stir in the reserved liquid and leave to cool. When cool, add the remaining yogurt and the tarragon. Season to taste with salt and pepper and mix thoroughly together.

■

11 GARNISH the turban with tarragon leaves and serve with the tarragon sauce.

■ SALADE NIÇOISE ■

There are many different versions of this famous French salad. This delicious version includes fresh tuna fish and sardines; the sardines are optional but worth including if you can find them.

SERVES 4–6

175 g (6 oz) small French beans
1 tuna steak, weighing about 275 g
  (10 oz)
45 ml (3 tbsp) olive oil
4 fresh sardines, scaled and cleaned (see
  page 10), optional
225 g (8 oz) ripe tomatoes
4 hard-boiled eggs

1 large crisp lettuce such as cos,
  Webb's wonder, batavia, radicchio
100 g (4 oz) black olives
50 g (2 oz) can anchovy fillets in olive
  oil
15 ml (1 tbsp) lemon juice
salt and pepper

■

1 TOP and tail the beans and put into a large shallow dish with 15 ml (1 tbsp) water. Cover and cook on HIGH for 2–3 minutes, until slightly softened, stirring once. Drain, rinse with cold water and put into a large salad bowl.

■

2 PUT the tuna into the shallow dish. Brush with some of the olive oil, cover and cook on HIGH for 3 minutes. Meanwhile, remove and discard the heads from the sardines. Cut the fish in half and arrange around the edge of the tuna. Brush with olive oil. Cook the tuna and sardines on HIGH for 1–2 minutes until tender.

■

3 REMOVE and discard the skin and bones from the tuna, flake the flesh and put into the salad bowl with the beans and sardines. Leave to cool.

■

4 WHEN the fish and beans are cold, quarter the tomatoes and hard-boiled eggs and tear the lettuce into large pieces. Add the tomatoes, eggs, lettuce and olives to the salad bowl and carefully mix everything together.

■

5 DRAIN the anchovy fillets, reserving the oil and mix into the salad. Whisk the anchovy oil, remaining olive oil, lemon juice and salt and pepper to taste together. Pour over the salad and toss together. Serve immediately with French bread.

· CIDER-SOUSED MACKEREL ·

These mackerel are delicious served with brown bread and butter for a light lunch dish.

SERVES 4

4 mackerel or herrings, each weighing
   about 275 g (10 oz), cleaned
salt and pepper
1 medium onion, skinned and very
   thinly sliced
150 ml (¼ pint) dry cider
45 ml (3 tbsp) cider or white wine
   vinegar

3 black peppercorns
2 allspice berries
2 cloves
2 bay leaves
½ a lemon, thinly sliced

·

1 FILLET the fish (see page 11), leaving the tails attached. Season the fillets with salt and pepper, then roll up each fillet towards the tail with the flesh side inside. Secure with cocktail sticks.

·

2 ARRANGE the fish around the edge of a shallow dish with the tails pointing upwards.

·

3 SCATTER the onion slices on top of the fish. Pour over the cider and vinegar and sprinkle with the remaining ingredients.

·

4 COVER and cook on HIGH for 7–8 minutes or until the fish is tender, basting occasionally. Leave to cool in the dish, basting occasionally with the cooking liquid.

· OCTOPUS STEWED IN RED WINE ·

Octopus needs to be tenderised before cooking. The easiest way to do this is to beat it vigorously with a meat mallet or a rolling pin. Marinating before cooking also helps to make it more tender.

SERVES 4–6

1.1 kg (2½ lb) octopus, cleaned (see
   page 11)
2 celery sticks, thinly sliced
1 large onion, skinned and sliced
3 garlic cloves, skinned and crushed
5 ml (1 level tsp) dried thyme
5 ml (1 level tsp) dried marjoram

5 ml (1 level tsp) ground cinnamon
5 ml (1 level tsp) sugar
30 ml (2 tbsp) olive oil
450 ml (¾ pint) dry red wine
salt and pepper
chopped fresh parsley, to garnish

1 To tenderise the octopus, beat it vigorously with a meat mallet or a rolling pin. Cut the body into thin strips and the tentacles into 2.5 cm (1 inch) pieces. Put into a large bowl with all the remaining ingredients, except the parsley, and leave to marinate for 2–3 hours.

■

2 WHEN ready to cook, cover and cook on HIGH for 5 minutes or until boiling, stirring once, then continue to cook on MEDIUM for 25–30 minutes or until the octopus is very tender. Leave to cool. Serve cold, garnished with chopped parsley.

■ *PIQUANT PURPLE SALAD* ■

This winter salad is so named because of its attractive combination of colours; the fish is coloured with flashes of purple by the beetroot and rests on a bed of dark red leaves.

SERVES 4

450 g (1 lb) baby new potatoes,
   scrubbed
60 ml (4 tbsp) olive oil
30 ml (2 tbsp) white wine vinegar
salt and pepper
450 g (1 lb) whiting fillets, skinned
30 ml (2 tbsp) milk
2 large pickled dill cucumbers or
   4 pickled gherkins

½ a cucumber
175 g (6 oz) cooked beetroot
selection of red salad leaves, such as
   radicchio, red lalola, oak leaf lettuce
30 ml (2 tbsp) capers
6 anchovy fillets
30 ml (2 tbsp) chopped fresh dill

■

1 PUT the potatoes into a medium bowl with 30 ml (2 tbsp) water. Cover and cook on HIGH for 8–10 minutes until tender, stirring occasionally.

■

2 WHILE the potatoes are cooking, make the dressing. Whisk the oil and vinegar together and season to taste with salt and pepper. When the potatoes are cooked, drain well and pour the dressing over them. Leave to cool.

■

3 CUT the fish into small strips about 1 cm (½ inch) wide and 7.5 cm (3 inches) long and put into a shallow dish with the milk. Cover and cook on HIGH for 3–4 minutes until just cooked. Do not overcook or the fish will break up and spoil the appearance of the salad. Leave to cool.

■

4 WHEN the potatoes and fish are cold, slice the pickled dill cucumbers or gherkins and the cucumber and mix with the potatoes. Peel the beetroot and cut into chunks.

■

5 ARRANGE the salad leaves on a serving platter. Spoon over the potato mixture, then the fish and then the beetroot. Mix lightly together. Sprinkle with the capers, anchovies and dill. Serve with crusty bread.

· CLASSIC FISH DISHES ·

This chapter contains a selection of classic fish dishes that adapt successfully to microwave cooking. For example, Poached Salmon and Sauce Hollandaise can be made very simply and quickly with little chance of failure if you follow the instructions on page 104 exactly. And for the classics of the Mediterranean – Plaki, La Bourride and Bouillabaise – the only thing lacking from the recipes is a little sunshine and a sea view!

· *SOLE À LA MEUNIÈRE* ·

It is essential to use unsalted butter for this dish since the salt particles in salted butter burn when heated.

SERVES 2

30 ml (2 level tbsp) plain flour
salt and pepper
4 sole fillets, each weighing about 75 g (3 oz), skinned

100 g (4 oz) unsalted butter
juice of ½ a lemon
lemon wedges and parsley sprigs, to garnish.

·

1 HEAT a browning dish on HIGH for 3–4 minutes or for about half the time recommended by the manufacturer. (Do not heat it too much or the butter will burn.)

·

2 SEASON the flour generously with salt and pepper, then dip the sole in the flour. Shake off the excess.

·

3 PUT half the butter into the browning dish and cook on HIGH for 30 seconds or until melted. Swirl to coat the base of the dish.

·

4 ADD the sole fillets and cook on HIGH for 1 minute. Turn over and cook on HIGH for 1 minute or until the fish just looks opaque.

5 TRANSFER the cooked sole fillets to a serving dish.

■

6 QUICKLY wipe out the browning dish with absorbent kitchen paper, then add the remaining butter and the lemon juice and cook on HIGH for 2–3 minutes or until hot and bubbling (do not overcook or the butter will burn). Pour over the fish, garnish with lemon wedges and parsley and serve immediately.

■ *SOLE VÉRONIQUE* ■

It is essential to peel the grapes for this dish. They can be peeled in advance and then stored, covered, in the refrigerator until required.

SERVES 4

2 shallots, skinned and very finely
    chopped
200 ml (7 fl oz) dry white wine
8 sole fillets, each weighing about 75 g
    (3 oz), skinned
225 g (8 oz) small seedless white
    grapes

2 egg yolks
25 g (1 oz) butter
45 ml (3 tbsp) double cream
salt and white pepper

■

1 PUT the shallots and wine into a large shallow dish. Cover and cook on HIGH for 3–4 minutes until the shallots are very soft.

■

2 FOLD the sole fillets in half with the skinned side inwards, and arrange in a single layer in the dish with the wine and shallots. Re-cover and cook on HIGH for 5–6 minutes or until the fish is tender.

■

3 MEANWHILE, peel the grapes and cut in half.

■

4 WHEN the fish is cooked, transfer it to a serving dish. Stir the egg yolks, butter and cream into the cooking liquid and mix well together. Cook on MEDIUM for 2–3 minutes or until slightly thickened, stirring occasionally. Do not allow the sauce to boil or it will curdle.

■

5 STIR in half the grapes and cook on MEDIUM for 1 minute or until hot. Season to taste with salt and white pepper.

■

6 POUR over the fish, decorate with the remaining grapes and serve immediately.

· POACHED SALMON WITH SAUCE HOLLANDAISE ·

Sauce Hollandaise is the classic fish sauce — but it can be difficult to make as it curdles very easily. Follow these instructions exactly and you will achieve perfect results every time.

SERVES 4

4 salmon steaks, each weighing about
   225 g (8 oz)
60 ml (4 tbsp) medium dry white wine
100 g (4 oz) butter, cut into small
   pieces

2 egg yolks
30 ml (2 tbsp) white wine vinegar
white pepper

·

1 ARRANGE the salmon with the thinner ends pointing towards the centre in a large shallow dish. Pour over the wine, cover and cook on HIGH for 6–8 minutes or until tender. Leave to stand, covered, while making the sauce.

·

2 To make the sauce, put the butter into a large glass bowl and cook on HIGH for 30–60 seconds until just melted (do not cook for any longer or the butter will be too hot and the mixture will curdle).

·

3 ADD the egg yolks and the vinegar and whisk together until well mixed. Cook on HIGH for 1–1½ minutes, whisking every 15 seconds until thick enough to coat the back of a spoon. Season with a little pepper.

·

4 TRANSFER the salmon to four serving plates and serve immediately with the sauce.

· TROUT WITH ALMONDS ·

A simple but delicious combination. If you haven't got fresh dill, use parsley or chives instead.

SERVES 2

2 trout, each weighing about 225 g
   (8 oz), cleaned (see page 10)
15 ml (1 level tbsp) plain flour
salt and pepper
15 ml (1 tbsp) vegetable oil

25 g (1 oz) butter or margarine
25 g (1 oz) flaked almonds
15 ml (1 tbsp) lemon juice
15 ml (1 tbsp) chopped fresh dill

·

1 HEAT a browning dish on HIGH for 5–8 minutes or according to manufacturer's instructions.

2 MEANWHILE, wipe the trout and cut off their heads just behind the gills. Season the flour with salt and pepper and use to coat the fish.

■

3 PUT the oil into the browning dish, then quickly add the fish. Cook on HIGH for 2 minutes, then turn over and cook on HIGH for 2 minutes, or until the fish is tender. Transfer the fish to a serving dish.

■

4 QUICKLY wipe out the browning dish with kitchen paper, then add the butter or margarine, and the almonds and cook on HIGH for 2–3 minutes or until lightly browned, stirring occasionally.

■

5 STIR in the lemon juice, dill, salt and pepper and cook on HIGH for 1 minute or until hot. Pour over the trout and serve immediately.

■ *FISH PLAKI* ■

Plaki is the traditional Greek method for cooking whole fish with lemon and tomato. In Greece it is baked in the oven, but it adapts well to cooking in the microwave. Serve with plain boiled potatoes.

SERVES 4

10 ml (2 level tsp) coriander seeds
10 ml (2 level tsp) fennel seeds
1 garlic clove, skinned and crushed
1 medium onion, skinned and finely
  chopped
30 ml (2 tbsp) olive oil
397 g (14 oz) can tomatoes
30 ml (2 tbsp) chopped fresh parsley

150 ml (¼ pint) dry white wine
salt and pepper
1.4 kg (3 lb) fat whole fish, such as
  bream, brill, John Dory, red mullet
  or grey mullet, scaled and cleaned
1 lemon
chopped fresh parsley, to garnish

■

1 CRUSH the coriander and fennel seeds in a pestle and mortar and put into a medium bowl with the garlic, onion, olive oil, tomatoes, parsley and wine. Cook on HIGH for about 12 minutes or until sauce is reduced and slightly thickened. Season to taste with salt and pepper.

■

2 MEANWHILE, using a sharp knife remove the head and tail from the fish and discard. Slash the fish two or three times on each side, and place in a large dish.

■

3 POUR the sauce over the fish. Slice the lemon very thinly and arrange on top of the sauce. Cover and cook on HIGH for 9–12 minutes or until the fish is tender (the time will depend on the thickness of the fish).

■

4 GARNISH with chopped parsley and serve straight from the dish with boiled potatoes.

▪ *MACKEREL WITH GOOSEBERRY SAUCE* ▪

The sharp tangy gooseberry sauce makes the perfect accompaniment to mackerel. If you prefer a less sharp sauce, add a little more sugar.

SERVES 2

175 g (6 oz) gooseberries, topped and
   tailed
15 ml (1 level tbsp) caster sugar
15 g (½ oz) butter or margarine
salt and pepper

grated nutmeg
2 mackerel, each weighing about 350 g
   (12 oz), cleaned (see page 10)
15 ml (1 tbsp) vegetable oil

▪

1 To make the sauce, put the gooseberries, sugar, butter or margarine and 45 ml (3 tbsp) water into a medium bowl. Cover and cook on HIGH for 4–5 minutes until the gooseberries are softened, stirring once.

▪

2 PURÉE in a blender or food processor, then return to the rinsed-out bowl. Season well with pepper and nutmeg and add a little salt.

▪

3 USING a sharp knife, slash the fish three times on each side. Arrange in a shallow dish and brush with the oil. Cover and cook on HIGH for 5–6 minutes or until the fish is cooked.

▪

4 REHEAT the sauce on HIGH for 2 minutes or until hot. Serve the fish with a little of the sauce poured over and the remainder handed separately.

▪ *RAIE AU BEURRE NOIR* ▪

Skate is a flavoursome fish that is good to eat because it has no small bones.

SERVES 2

75 g (3 oz) unsalted butter
30 ml (2 tbsp) white wine vinegar
30 ml (2 tbsp) capers (optional)
1 skate wing, weighing about 700 g
   (1½ lb)

1 small onion, skinned and sliced
30 ml (2 tbsp) chopped fresh parsley
salt and pepper

▪

1 CUT the butter into small pieces and put into a medium bowl. Cover and cook on HIGH for 4–5 minutes until light brown (do not overcook or the butter will burn). Carefully add half the vinegar and the capers, if using, and cook for a further 1 minute until hot. Set aside.

▪

2 CUT the skate in half and put into a large shallow dish with the onion and remaining vinegar. Pour over about 150 ml (¼ pint) water, then cover and cook on HIGH for 9–10 minutes or until the fish is tender.

3 REMOVE the fish from the stock and arrange on two plates. Sprinkle with the parsley and salt and pepper to taste. Cook the sauce on HIGH for 1 minute to reheat. Pour over the fish and serve immediately.

▪ *BOUILLABAISSE* ▪

Bouillabaisse is another classic Mediterranean fish soup and although it should contain the rascasse, a fish not found outside the Mediterranean, it is possible to make an acceptable bouillabaisse if you make every effort to include as many different kinds of seafood as possible. Other essentials are large bowls of aioli or rouille and plenty of French bread and wine.

SERVES 6

4 large tomatoes, skinned
1 leek
1 medium onion, skinned
½ a small fennel bulb
1 small red chilli
few sprigs of parsley
150 ml (¼ pint) olive oil
large pinch of saffron strands

4 garlic cloves, skinned and crushed
1.8 kg (4 lb) fish such as red mullet, monkfish, conger eel, John Dory, cooked langoustines or fresh mussels, cleaned (see page 12)
salt and pepper
Aioli (see page 125) or Rouille (see page 121), to serve

▪

1 ROUGHLY chop the tomatoes, leek, onion and fennel and put into the largest bowl you have (make sure it will fit into the cooker first!). Add the whole chilli, parsley, oil, saffron and garlic, then pour over about 1.7 litres (3 pints) boiling water.

▪

2 COVER and cook on HIGH for 8–10 minutes until the water is boiling rapidly and the vegetables are softened, stirring once.

▪

3 WHILE the vegetables are cooking, clean and scale the fish if necessary and cut into large chunks (removing the heads and tails if desired). Leave the red mullet whole if small.

▪

4 ADD the thickest fish to the soup and the red mullet if cooking whole, and cook on HIGH for 4–5 minutes or until almost cooked, then add any thinner pieces of fish and the langoustines or mussels. Cook on HIGH for a further 4–5 minutes or until all the fish is cooked, stirring occasionally but being careful not to break up the fish.

▪

5 USING a slotted spoon, quickly remove the fish and arrange in a serving dish. Leave the langoustines or mussels in their shells. Strain the soup and season with salt and pepper, then pour into a hot soup tureen. Serve immediately with the fish and the aioli or rouille.

▪ *SEAFOOD GUMBO* ▪

Gumbo is a Creole dish invented by the French settlers of Louisiana. It is really a hearty soup containing okra and lots of seafood, and was originally thickened with filé powder, a substance made from the leaves of the sassafras tree. It is always served in bowls with boiled rice.

SERVES 6

1 large onion, skinned and chopped
1–2 garlic cloves, skinned and crushed
25 g (1 oz) butter or margarine
15 ml (1 level tbsp) plain flour
900 ml (1½ pints) boiling fish or
    vegetable stock (see pages 125 and
    123)
4 large tomatoes, skinned and chopped
1 green pepper, seeded and chopped
225 g (8 oz) okra, trimmed and sliced

15 ml (1 tbsp) tomato purée
grated rind of 1 lemon
225 g (8 oz) cooked peeled prawns
225 g (8 oz) cooked crab meat (see
    page 13)
6 large shelled scallops
Tabasco sauce
salt and pepper
boiled rice, to serve

▪

1 PUT the onion, garlic and butter or margarine into a large bowl. Cover and cook on HIGH for 3–4 minutes until slightly softened.

▪

2 SPRINKLE in the flour and cook on HIGH for 1 minute, then gradually add the stock, stirring all the time. Add the tomatoes, pepper, okra, tomato purée and lemon rind, re-cover and cook on HIGH for 6–7 minutes or until the okra is tender, stirring occasionally.

▪

3 ADD the remaining ingredients and season to taste with Tabasco sauce and salt and pepper. Re-cover and cook on HIGH for 4–5 minutes or until the scallops are cooked and the prawns and crab meat are heated through, stirring occasionally.

▪

4 To serve, spoon some boiled rice into six large soup bowls and ladle the gumbo on top. Serve immediately.

▪ *LA BOURRIDE* ▪

La bourride is a famous dish of Provençe. Many versions can be found in cookery books and restaurants but the essential ingredient is the aioli or garlic mayonnaise which is added to the hot stock after the fish is cooked. Here is a simple version.

SERVES 4

900 ml (1½ pints) fish or vegetable
    stock (see pages 125 and 123)
4 white fish fillets, such as bass,
    turbot, monkfish, brill or John Dory

300 ml (½ pint) Aioli (see page 125)

Steak
with Blue Cheese Sauce

Serves 2
ready in 10 minutes
calories per serving 303
fat per serving 17.5g

ASDA

Steak
with Blue Cheese Sauce

ASDA has all you need...

2 ASDA lean rump steaks
(Approx. 2cm, (3/4") thick)
15ml (1tbsp) oil
25g (1oz) ASDA soft & creamy
cheese
25g (1oz) ASDA Italian
Dolcelatte or Stilton cheese,
crumbled
60ml (4tbsp) ASDA fresh
semi skimmed milk

Beef

to go with your meal

ASDA CHATEAUNEUF-DU-PAPE
75cl £9.95
Taste Guide D
Why not treat yourself
to something special -
a steak deserves it.
Châteauneuf is the
most famous region
within the Côtes du
Rhône, it produces top
quality chunky, spicy
red wines.

step by step...

1   Heat the oil in a large non-stick frying pan and cook the steaks according to the timings below.

2   Add the soft cream cheese, Dolcelatte or Stilton and milk to the pan and gently heat for 1 minute until melted.

3   Serve the steak and sauce with chunky oven baked chips, crusty bread and mixed salad leaves.

cooking instructions

Use these timings as a guide when cooking your steaks:
Rare - 2 minutes per side
Medium - 4 minutes per side
Well done - 6 minutes per side

for even more delicious family meal ideas see the current issue of

1 Pour the stock into a large wide bowl and cook on HIGH for 15–20 minutes until reduced by about one third. Meanwhile, cut the fillets in half if large.

■

2 Carefully lower the fish into the stock and cook on HIGH for 4–8 minutes until tender (the time will depend on the thickness of the fish). Remove the fish with a slotted spoon and arrange in four large soup bowls.

■

3 Put the aioli into a bowl and gradually whisk a little of the hot stock into it. Pour the aioli mixture into the remaining stock and cook on HIGH for 1–2 minutes until just heated through. Do not allow the mixture to boil or it will curdle.

■

4 Pour the stock over the fish and serve immediately, with lots of bread or boiled new potatoes.

■ *MOULES MARINIÈRE* ■

This typical French recipe is the simplest method for cooking mussels.

SERVES 2 (AS A LIGHT MEAL)

1 small onion, skinned and finely chopped
1 garlic clove, skinned and crushed
150 ml (¼ pint) dry white wine
15 ml (1 tbsp) chopped fresh parsley

900 g (2 lb) fresh mussels, cleaned (see page 12)
25 g (1 oz) butter
salt and pepper
chopped fresh parsley, to garnish

■

1 Put the onion, garlic, wine, parsley and 45 ml (3 tbsp) water in a large bowl and cook on HIGH for 2–3 minutes or until hot.

■

2 Stir in the mussels, cover and cook on HIGH for 3–5 minutes or until all of the mussels have opened, removing the mussels on the top as they open and shaking the bowl occasionally. Discard any mussels which do not open.

■

3 Strain the mussels through a sieve and return the cooking liquid to the bowl. Put the mussels into two large soup bowls.

■

4 Cut the butter into small pieces and stir into the cooking liquid. Cook on HIGH for 1–2 minutes or until hot, stirring frequently. Season to taste.

■

5 Pour the sauce over the mussels. Garnish with plenty of chopped parsley and serve immediately with French bread to mop up the juices.

• *COQUILLES SAINT JACQUES* •

Coquilles saint Jacques is French for scallops, but in England it has become a term to describe various mixtures of scallops and sauce which are cooked and then served in the scallop shells.

SERVES 6 (AS A STARTER)

25 g (1 oz) plain flour
25 g (1 oz) butter
300 ml (½ pint) milk
8 large shelled scallops (shells reserved)

50 g (2 oz) button mushrooms
50 g (2 oz) Gruyère cheese, grated
salt and pepper

■

1 PUT the flour, butter and milk into a medium bowl and cook on HIGH for 3–4 minutes or until the sauce is thickened, stirring frequently.

■

2 MEANWHILE, prepare the scallops. Remove and discard from each scallop the tough white 'muscle' which is found opposite the coral. Separate the corals from the scallops. Thinly slice the scallops and leave the corals whole. Thinly slice the mushrooms.

■

3 STIR the sliced scallops and mushrooms into the sauce and cook on HIGH for 1–2 minutes or until almost cooked, stirring once. Add the corals and cook on HIGH for about 1 minute or until the scallops and corals are cooked.

■

4 STIR in half the cheese and salt and pepper to taste. Spoon the mixture into six of the scallop shells or six small gratin dishes. Sprinkle with the remaining cheese and brown under a hot grill. Serve immediately.

• *LA MOUCLADE* •

When mussels are cooked and then served on the half shell they are called mouclade. Here they are served in a delicious cream and garlic sauce.

SERVES 2 (AS A LIGHT MEAL)

900 g (2 lb) fresh mussels, cleaned (see
    page 12)
150 ml (¼ pint) dry white wine
1 small onion, skinned and finely
    chopped
1 garlic clove, skinned and crushed

150 ml (¼ pint) double cream
15 ml (1 tbsp) lemon juice
pinch of ground turmeric
salt and pepper
1 egg yolk
chopped fresh parsley, to garnish

■

1 PUT the mussels, wine and onion into a large bowl, cover and cook on HIGH for 3–5 minutes or until the mussels have opened, removing the mussels on the top as they open and shaking the bowl occasionally. Discard any mussels which do not open.

2 STRAIN the mussels through a sieve and return the cooking liquid to the bowl. Discard one half shell from each mussel and keep the mussels warm while making the sauce.

■

3 STIR the garlic into the reserved cooking liquid and cook on HIGH for 5–6 minutes or until reduced by half. Stir in the cream, lemon juice, turmeric and season to taste with salt and pepper. Cook on HIGH for 2 minutes or until hot.

■

4 STIR in the egg yolk and cook on HIGH for 30 seconds or until slightly thickened, stirring once. Pour the sauce over the mussels, sprinkle with chopped parsley and serve immediately.

▪ *LOBSTER THERMIDOR* ▪

This famous restaurant dish is simple and easy to prepare at home. See page 12 for a detailed description of how to cook and prepare lobster.

SERVES 2

50 ml (2 oz) butter
1 small onion, skinned and very finely chopped
150 ml (¼ pint) dry white wine
150 ml (¼ pint) milk
25 g (1 oz) plain flour
2 cooked lobsters, each weighing about 450 g (1 lb) (see page 12)

45 ml (3 level tbsp) freshly grated Parmesan cheese
5 ml (1 tsp) French mustard
cayenne pepper
salt

■

1 PUT half the butter and the onion into a large bowl. Cover and cook on HIGH for 3–4 minutes until the onion is very soft.

■

2 ADD the wine, milk, flour and remaining butter and cook on HIGH for 2–3 minutes until the sauce is boiling and thickened, stirring frequently. Continue to cook on HIGH for 3 minutes, stirring occasionally.

■

3 MEANWHILE, cut the lobsters in half lengthways (see page 13). Remove the meat from the shells. Crack open the large claws and remove the flesh (leave the smaller claws attached). Chop the claw and head meat roughly and cut the tail meat into thick slices.

■

4 ADD the lobster meat, half the cheese and the mustard to the sauce and cook on HIGH for 2 minutes or until hot. Season to taste with cayenne pepper and salt, then pile the mixture back into the lobster shells. Sprinkle with the remaining cheese, then brown quickly under a hot grill. Serve immediately.

▪ *PAELLA* ▪

Spain's most famous dish, paella, gets its name from the pan in which it is traditionally cooked. There are many different recipes from each province of Spain but rice, onions, tomatoes, fish and shellfish and the Spanish sausage chorizo are always included.

SERVES 6–8

60 ml (4 tbsp) olive oil
1 medium onion, skinned and chopped
3 garlic cloves, skinned and crushed
450 g (1 lb) risotto rice
pinch of saffron strands
1.1 litres (2 pints) boiling fish or vegetable stock (see pages 125 and 123)
1 red or green pepper, seeded and chopped
350 g (12 oz) tomatoes, roughly chopped

100 g (4 oz) chorizo sausage, thickly sliced
450 g (1 lb) fish fillets such as monkfish, whiting or red bream, skinned
6 cooked langoustines or 225 g (8 oz) cooked peeled prawns
450 g (1 lb) fresh mussels, cleaned (see page 12)
paprika
salt and pepper
chopped fresh parsley, to garnish

▪

1 PUT the oil, onion and garlic into a large bowl. Cover and cook on HIGH for 2–3 minutes until the onion is slightly softened.

▪

2 ADD the rice and the saffron and stir until all of the rice is coated in the oil. Pour in the stock, re-cover and cook on HIGH for 12 minutes, stirring once.

▪

3 ADD the pepper, tomatoes and chorizo. Re-cover and continue to cook on HIGH for 3–5 minutes or until the rice is tender and most of the liquid is absorbed.

▪

4 CUT the fish into small chunks and lay on top of the rice. Lay the mussels and the langoustines or the prawns on top of the fish. If the rice is very dry sprinkle the fish with 30 ml (2 tbsp) water to create steam during cooking.

▪

5 COVER and cook on HIGH for 4–5 minutes or until the fish looks opaque and the mussels have opened. Discard any unopened mussels.

▪

6 SEASON generously with paprika and salt and pepper then mix carefully together. Transfer to a large serving platter or shallow dish. Sprinkle generously with parsley and serve immediately.

Opposite: *Piquant Purple Salad (page 101)*
Overleaf: *Raie au Beurre Noir (page 106)*

· ACCOMPANIMENTS ·

Having created a wonderful main course, you may be confronted with the problem of what to serve with it. Fish is notoriously difficult to choose an accompaniment for, but the following chapter provides a selection of interesting side dishes, all of which complement the flavour and texture of fish. Most, such as French Beans in Lime Butter or Grated Courgettes with Poppy Seeds take only a few minutes to cook and should be served immediately, so cook the main course and then quickly put the vegetables into the microwave to cook while you are serving the main course.

· *CABBAGE IN CARAWAY CREAM* ·

This creamy, spicy cabbage dish is the ideal accompaniment to simple fish dishes that do not have a sauce.

SERVES 4

45 ml (3 tbsp) vegetable oil
15 ml (1 level tbsp) caraway seeds
450 g (1 lb) savoy cabbage, shredded
150 ml (¼ pint) soured cream or Greek strained yogurt

10 ml (2 tsp) Dijon mustard
salt and pepper

·

1 PUT the oil into a medium bowl. Lightly crush the caraway seeds and add to the oil. Cook on HIGH for 3 minutes or until the oil is very hot and the caraway seeds begin to release a fragrant aroma.

·

2 ADD the cabbage, stir to coat in the oil and cook on HIGH for 2–3 minutes until the cabbage is tender but still crispy. (Cook for 1–2 minutes longer if you prefer less crispy cabbage, but do not cook until soggy.)

·

3 MIX the cream or yogurt and mustard together and toss to coat the cabbage. Cook on HIGH for 1 minute or until hot. Season generously with black pepper and a little salt and serve immediately.

▪ *CREAMED PARSLEY* ▪

Ring the changes with parsley as a vegetable – cooked this way it makes an unusual and interesting accompaniment.

SERVES 4

1 small onion, skinned and finely
  chopped
25 g (1 oz) butter or margarine
large bunch of parsley, weighing about
  175 g (6 oz)

150 ml (¼ pint) double cream or Greek
  strained yogurt
freshly grated nutmeg
salt and pepper

▪

1 PUT the onion and butter or margarine into a bowl, cover and cook on HIGH for 4–5 minutes or until the onion is softened.

▪

2 MEANWHILE, trim the parsley, discarding any tough stalks and discoloured leaves, then chop finely (use a food processor to save time).

▪

3 ADD the chopped parsley to the onion and cook on HIGH for 2–3 minutes or until the parsley is softened, stirring occasionally. Do not overcook or the parsley will loose its colour.

▪

4 STIR in the cream or yogurt and season generously with nutmeg, pepper and a little salt. Cook on HIGH for 1 minute or until hot and serve immediately.

▪ *GRATED COURGETTES WITH POPPY SEEDS* ▪

Adapt this simple and delicious method of cooking for other vegetables such as carrots, celeriac and parsnips (increasing the cooking time by 2–3 minutes). It is essential to ensure that the remainder of the meal is ready when you start to cook this dish as it must be served straight from the microwave.

SERVES 4

30 ml (2 tbsp) olive oil
30 ml (2 tbsp) black poppy seeds
1 garlic clove, skinned and crushed

450 g (1 lb) courgettes
salt and pepper

▪

1 PUT the oil, poppy seeds and garlic into a browning dish or shallow dish and cook on HIGH for 2–3 minutes or until very hot, stirring once.

▪

2 MEANWHILE, coarsely grate the courgettes in a food processor or using a mandolin. When the oil is hot, quickly add the courgettes and cook on HIGH for 2 minutes or until very hot, stirring occasionally. Season to taste with salt and pepper and serve immediately.

• BRAISED FENNEL •

Fennel is the classic accompaniment for fish. Always try to buy bulbs with green feathery leaves, so you can use the leaves as a garnish.

SERVES 4

2 large fennel bulbs, each weighing
   about 450 g (1 lb)
1 bouquet garni
30 ml (2 tbsp) olive oil

salt and pepper
30 ml (2 level tbsp) freshly grated
   Parmesan cheese

1 TRIM the fennel, discarding any discoloured or bruised parts. Reserve any green feathery leaves for the garnish.

2 DIVIDE the fennel into quarters, then cut each quarter several times lengthways, leaving the root end intact. Pull the slices slightly apart to make fans. Arrange around the edge of a large shallow flameproof dish with the root ends towards the outside. Add the bouquet garni, then pour over 30 ml (2 tbsp) water and the olive oil, then cover and cook on HIGH for about 15 minutes or until the fennel is tender.

3 SEASON with the salt and pepper, then sprinkle with the Parmesan cheese and brown under a hot grill. Chop the reserved fennel leaves and sprinkle on top of the fennel to garnish. Serve immediately.

• FRENCH BEANS IN LIME BUTTER •

French beans are the perfect accompaniment for fish, giving a good contrast in texture and colour. They should be cooked lightly until just tender but still crisp.

SERVES 4

finely grated rind and juice of 1 lime
50 g (2 oz) butter

700 g (1½ lb) French beans, trimmed
salt and pepper

1 PUT the lime rind and juice and the butter into a medium bowl. Cover and cook on HIGH for 2 minutes or until the butter is melted and the lime rind is slightly softened, stirring once.

2 ADD the beans and stir to coat in the butter. Re-cover and cook on HIGH for 3–4 minutes or until the beans are softened, but still retain some 'bite' and their bright green colour.

3 SEASON to taste with salt and pepper and serve immediately with plain fish dishes.

APPLE AND BRAZIL NUT STUFFED MUSHROOMS ·

Stuffed mushrooms look very pretty and are easy to make. Choose the large cup or flat black variety of mushrooms – don't be tempted to stuff button mushrooms! The fruit and nut stuffing used here goes particularly well with oily fish such as mackerel.

SERVES 2–4

1 medium onion, skinned and finely chopped
45 ml (3 tbsp) nut or olive oil
1 small apple, peeled and finely chopped
50 g (2 oz) shelled Brazil nuts, finely chopped

juice of ½ a small lemon
salt and pepper
4 large cup mushrooms
fresh chives, to garnish

1 PUT the onion and 15 ml (1 tbsp) of the oil into a small bowl. Cover and cook on HIGH for 5 minutes until the onion is soft.

2 ADD the apple, Brazil nuts and lemon juice and season to taste with salt and pepper. Re-cover and cook on HIGH for 2 minutes.

3 MEANWHILE, brush the mushrooms with the remaining oil and arrange, stalk side up, in a shallow dish.

4 SPOON the stuffing on top of the mushrooms and sprinkle with the chives. Cook on HIGH for 3–4 minutes or until the mushrooms are just tender. Serve immediately.

INDIVIDUAL HERB POTATO LAYERS ·

Make sure that you grease the ramekins thoroughly or the mixture will stick.

SERVES 4

450 g (1 lb) potatoes
150 ml (¼ pint) milk
2 eggs
1 garlic clove, skinned and crushed (optional)

60 ml (4 tbsp) chopped fresh mixed herbs, such as chives, parsley, chervil and tarragon
salt and pepper

1 PEEL the potatoes and, using a very sharp knife, slice them as thinly as possible.

2 BEAT the milk, eggs, garlic and half the herbs together and season generously with salt and pepper.

3 GREASE four 150 ml (¼ pint) ramekin dishes and line the bases with greaseproof paper. Grease the paper.

▪

4 SPRINKLE the remaining herbs into the base of each ramekin and pour over a thin layer of flavoured milk. Arrange a layer of potatoes on top. Keep repeating the layers and pouring over the milk, pushing the potatoes down well, until each dish is full.

▪

5 ARRANGE the ramekins in a circle on the turntable or base of the cooker and cover with a large plate. Cook on MEDIUM for about 15 minutes or until the potatoes are tender.

▪

6 LEAVE to stand for 2 minutes, then carefully loosen around the edge of each dish, turn out and serve immediately.

▪ *CELERIAC PURÉE* ▪

Celeriac has a delicious celery flavour and aroma, and when puréed with cream it makes a delicious accompaniment for fish. It does lack colour, so choose a garnish which complements the fish dish it is being served with – try chopped herbs, chopped nuts, or paprika.

SERVES 4–6

15 ml (1 tbsp) lemon juice
450 g (1 lb) celeriac
25 g (1 oz) butter or margarine

150 ml (¼ pint) single cream or Greek strained yogurt
salt and pepper

▪

1 FILL a medium bowl with cold water and add the lemon juice. Peel the celeriac and cut into 2.5 cm (1 inch) cubes, dropping them into the bowl of acidulated water as they are prepared, to prevent discoloration.

▪

2 DRAIN the celeriac and return to the bowl with 30 ml (2 tbsp) water. Cover and cook on HIGH for 6–7 minutes or until soft, stirring occasionally.

▪

3 DRAIN the celeriac and put into a blender or food processor with the butter or margarine and cream or yogurt and purée until smooth. Season to taste with salt and pepper.

▪

4 TURN the purée into a serving dish, cover and cook on HIGH for 2–3 minutes until hot. Garnish appropriately (see introduction) and serve immediately.

▪ *SPINACH WITH PINE NUTS* ▪

This classic combination of spinach and pine nuts goes well with most tomato-based fish dishes.

SERVES 4

50 g (2 oz) pine nuts
900 g (2 lb) fresh spinach or 450 g (1 lb) frozen spinach

25 g (1 oz) butter or margarine
salt and pepper

▪

1 SPREAD the pine nuts out on a large plate and cook on HIGH for 4–5 minutes until lightly toasted, stirring occasionally.

▪

2 MEANWHILE, remove any tough stems from the fresh spinach, chop roughly and put into a bowl. When the nuts are toasted, cover the spinach and cook on HIGH for 8–10 or until tender, stirring once. If using frozen spinach, put into a bowl, cover and cook on HIGH for 10–12 minutes until thawed, stirring frequently. Drain thoroughly and return to the bowl.

▪

3 ADD the pine nuts and the butter or margarine to the spinach and season to taste with salt and pepper. Cook on HIGH for 2–3 minutes or until very hot, stirring once. Serve immediately.

▪ *BABY BAKED POTATOES* ▪

Baked potatoes were the original accompaniment to fried fish in Britain because both were sold by street sellers. It was not until chips were introduced from the continent that fish and chips became the popular dish it still is today.

SERVES 4

8 potatoes, each weighing 100 g (4 oz)
salt and pepper

savoury butter (see page 122), optional

▪

1 WASH the potatoes thoroughly. Using a sharp knife, make three deep cuts from the top of each potato through to the middle.

▪

2 ARRANGE the potatoes, cut side down, in a circle on the turntable or the base of the cooker, and cook on HIGH for 12–15 minutes or until the potatoes are tender.

▪

3 To serve, turn the potatoes, cut side up, pull the slices apart and season with salt and pepper. Serve plain or topped with a savoury butter of your choice.

· SAMPHIRE WITH BUTTER ·

Samphire or sea asparagus is sometimes sold in fishmongers, and it makes a delicious and attractive accompaniment to fish dishes. It isn't really a seaweed, but a plant that has adapted to living in shallow sea areas. Eat it by biting the soft parts away from the harder parts.

SERVES 4

225 g (8 oz) samphire or sea asparagus   black pepper
25 g (1 oz) butter

·

1 WASH the samphire in several changes of water, then put into a medium bowl with 30 ml (2 tbsp) water. Cover and cook on HIGH for 4–6 minutes or until just tender, stirring occasionally.

·

2 DRAIN the samphire, cut the butter into small pieces and mix with the samphire. Toss together to coat in the butter. Season with black pepper and serve immediately.

· SIMPLE POTATO SALAD ·

A simple potato salad, served just warm and flavoured with the herbs of your choice, is a good accompaniment for fish and makes a change from the more usual chipped or boiled potatoes.

SERVES 4

700 g (1½ lb) small potatoes, scrubbed   30 ml (2 tbsp) chopped fresh herbs such
45 ml (3 tbsp) olive oil   as chervil, parsley or chives
15 ml (1 tbsp) white wine vinegar or   salt and pepper
   lemon juice

·

1 CUT the potatoes in half and put into a medium bowl with 45 ml (3 tbsp) water. Cover and cook on HIGH for 12–14 minutes or until the potatoes are tender, stirring occasionally.

·

2 WHILE the potatoes are cooking, put the oil, vinegar or lemon juice, herbs and salt and pepper to taste into a small bowl and whisk thoroughly together.

·

3 DRAIN the potatoes, then pour over the dressing and stir until all the potatoes are coated. Leave to stand for about 15 minutes to let the potatoes absorb the flavour, then serve while still warm. If preferred, make the salad in advance and before serving cook on HIGH for 2 minutes or until just warm.

▪ *BROAD BEANS WITH SAVORY* ▪

*Small, young broad beans are most suited to this method of cooking because
they are the most tender. As they get older the beans develop a thin,
parchment-like skin which slows down the cooking. If however you cannot
find any fresh beans use frozen and cook on HIGH for the same time.*

SERVES 4–6

1.1 kg (2½ lb) small young broad beans
few sprigs of savory

25 g (1 oz) butter or margarine
salt and pepper

▪

1 SHELL the beans and put into a large bowl with one sprig of savory
and 45 ml (3 tbsp) water. Cover and cook on HIGH for 6–10 minutes or
until the beans are just tender, stirring occasionally. (The time will
depend on the age of the beans.)

▪

2 MEANWHILE, chop the remaining savory. Cut the butter or margarine
into small pieces and mix with the savory.

▪

3 DRAIN the beans and remove and discard the savory sprig. (If you are
using older beans, you may need to remove their skins). Add the butter
or margarine and toss together so that the butter melts. Season with salt
and pepper. Cook on HIGH for 1–2 minutes to reheat if necessary, and
serve immediately.

▪ *HOT LEMON AND HERB BREAD* ▪

This delicious bread makes a good accompaniment for fish salads and soups.

SERVES 4

50 g (2 oz) butter or margarine
finely grated rind and juice of 1 small
    lemon
30 ml (2 tbsp) chopped fresh mixed
    herbs

salt and pepper
1 small baguette

▪

1 PUT the butter or margarine into a small bowl and cook on HIGH for
10–30 seconds or until just soft enough to spread. Beat in the lemon rind
and juice and the herbs and season to taste with salt and pepper.

▪

2 CUT the bread into 2.5 cm (1 inch) slices and spread both sides of each
slice with the butter. Stick the slices back together to re-form the loaf.

▪

3 WRAP in greaseproof paper and cook on HIGH for 1–2 minutes or
until the bread is hot. Serve immediately.

STOCKS, SAUCES AND SAVOURY BUTTERS ·

As well as the essential stock, this chapter contains a selection of recipes that can be used to enhance or complement the flavour of cooked fish dishes. Some, such as Bouillabaisse or Bourride, are traditionally served with Aioli or Rouille and you will find the recipes for these delicious Mediterranean sauces here. They are perfect for turning something bland into a dish full of flavour – try stirring a spoonful or two into your favourite fish stew, soup, salad or pilaff. I have also given recipes for Savoury Butters, Tomato Sauce and the ubiquitous white sauce with its many variations. These are all perfect for serving with plainly cooked fish or shellfish of your choice. Turn to page 14 for instructions and timings for cooking fish.

· *ROUILLE* ·

Rouille is a strongly flavoured sauce which is the classic accompaniment to many Mediterranean fish dishes. It is most successful if made using a blender or a pestle and mortar – the quantity is too small to be made in a food processor.

Makes about 200 ml (⅓ pint)

2 garlic cloves, peeled
2 red peppers, halved, seeded and chopped
2 slices white bread, crusts removed

30 ml (2 tbsp) olive oil
about 200 ml (⅓ pint) fish or vegetable stock (see pages 125 and 123)

·

1 Purée the garlic and the peppers together in a blender or pestle and mortar until completely smooth.

·

2 Soak the bread in a little water, then squeeze dry. Add to the pepper mixture and blend until smooth.

·

3 Gradually beat in the olive oil, then enough of the fish or vegetable stock to give a consistency similar to mayonnaise. Use immediately or store in the refrigerator for up to 1 week.

▪ *SAVOURY BUTTERS* ▪

Savoury butters make a delicious accompaniment for fish, and are quicker and easier to prepare than a sauce. Make a few hours before serving to allow time for the flavours to blend. Allow about 25 g (1 oz) per person.

100 g (4 oz) butter   salt and pepper

▪

1 PUT the butter in a small bowl and cook on HIGH for 1 minute or until softened but not melted.

▪

2 BEAT in one of the following flavourings and season with salt and pepper unless otherwise stated:

ANCHOVY BUTTER   6 anchovies, mashed with a fork. Do not add salt.

CRAB BUTTER   30 ml (2 tbsp) crab meat, 5 ml (1 tsp) lemon juice, cayenne pepper.

GARLIC BUTTER   2 garlic cloves, skinned and crushed, and 5–10 ml (1–2 tsp) chopped fresh parsley.

GOLDEN BUTTER   Sieved yolks of 2 hard-boiled eggs.

GREEN BUTTER   50 g (2 oz) chopped watercress.

GREEN PEPPERCORN BUTTER   15 ml (1 tbsp) crushed green peppercorns.

HORSERADISH BUTTER   30 ml (2 level tbsp) creamed horseradish.

LEMON OR LIME BUTTER   5 ml (1 tsp) finely grated lemon or lime rind and a squeeze of juice.

LOBSTER BUTTER   50 g (2 oz) lobster coral.

LUMPFISH ROE BUTTER   15–30 ml (1–2 tbsp) black or red lumpfish roe and 5 ml (1 tsp) lemon juice pounded together, then added to the butter. Do not add salt.

MAITRE D'HOTEL (PARSLEY) BUTTER   30 ml (2 tbsp) finely chopped fresh parsley and a squeeze of lemon juice, with salt and cayenne pepper.

ONION BUTTER   30 ml (2 level tbsp) finely grated onion.

SARDINE BUTTER   4 sardines, mashed with a fork, and few drops Worcestershire sauce.

TOMATO BUTTER   30 ml (2 level tbsp) tomato ketchup or 10 ml (2 level tsp) tomato purée and 5 ml (1 level tsp) sugar.

TARRAGON BUTTER   30 ml (2 tbsp) chopped fresh tarragon.

▪

3 SHAPE into a small roll, wrap in greaseproof paper and chill until firm. Serve cut into slices.

▪ *TOMATO SAUCE* ▪

Serve this simple tomato sauce with any plainly cooked fish, (follow the chart on page 14). The sauce can be made in advance and reheated before serving.

MAKES ABOUT 450 ML (¾ PINT)

30 ml (2 tbsp) olive oil
1 large onion, skinned and finely
    chopped
1 celery stick, trimmed and finely
    chopped
1 garlic clove, skinned and crushed
450 g (1 lb) ripe tomatoes, skinned,
    seeded and chopped or 397 g (14 oz)
    can tomatoes

150 ml (¼ pint) vegetable stock (see
    below)
15 ml (1 tbsp) tomato purée
5 ml (1 level tsp) sugar
salt and pepper

▪

1 PUT the oil, onion, celery and garlic in a large bowl. Cover and cook on HIGH for 5–7 minutes or until the vegetables are very soft.

▪

2 STIR in the chopped fresh tomatoes or canned tomatoes with their juice, the stock, tomato purée and sugar. Season to taste with salt and pepper. Cook on HIGH for 10 minutes or until the sauce is reduced and thickened, stirring occasionally.

▪

3 PURÉE in a blender or food processor, pour back into the bowl and cook on HIGH for 2 minutes or until hot.

▪ *VEGETABLE STOCK* ▪

This basic stock can be used in place of fish stock if preferred. It is not necessary to use the vegetables given here, it can be made with any vegetables that are available.

MAKES ABOUT 900 ML (1½ PINTS)

2 medium carrots
2 medium onions
3 celery sticks
2 leeks

4 juniper berries
bouquet garni
salt and pepper

▪

1 FINELY chop all of the vegetables (including the skins) and put into a large bowl with all the remaining ingredients. Pour over 1.1 litres (2 pints) boiling water. Cover and cook on HIGH for 20–30 minutes or until the vegetables are very soft.

▪

2 STRAIN through a sieve and adjust the seasoning if necessary. Cool, then store in the refrigerator until required.

▪ *WHITE SAUCE* ▪

*White sauce is a quick basic sauce with many variations. Serve with any
plainly cooked fish (follow the chart on page 14 to cook the fish).*

MAKES ABOUT 300 ML (½ PINT)

15 g (½ oz) butter or margarine   *salt and pepper*
15 g (½ oz) plain flour
300 ml (½ pint) milk, fish or vegetable
 stock (see pages 125 and 123)

▪

1 PUT all the ingredients in an ovenproof jug or small bowl and blend
well together.

▪

2 COOK on HIGH for 4–5 minutes or until the sauce has boiled and
thickened, stirring frequently.

VARIATIONS

Add the following to the hot sauce:

CHEESE SAUCE 50 g (2 oz) grated mature Cheddar cheese and a pinch of
mustard powder.

PARSLEY SAUCE 30 ml (2 tbsp) chopped fresh parsley.

HOT TARTARE SAUCE 15 ml (1 tbsp) chopped fresh parsley, 10 ml (2 level
tsp) chopped gherkins, 10 ml (2 level tsp) chopped capers and 15 ml
(1 tbsp) lemon juice.

CAPER SAUCE 15 ml (1 level tbsp) capers and 5–10 ml (1–2 tsp) vinegar
from the jar of capers.

BLUE CHEESE SAUCE 50 g (2 oz) crumbled Stilton or other blue cheese and
10 ml (2 tsp) lemon juice.

MUSHROOM SAUCE 75 g (3 oz) sliced, lightly cooked mushrooms.

ONION SAUCE 1 chopped cooked onion.

EGG SAUCE 1 finely chopped hard-boiled egg.

MUSTARD SAUCE 15–30 ml (1–2 tbsp) mild wholegrain mustard and a
squeeze of lemon juice.

ANCHOVY SAUCE Anchovy purée, to taste.

· *FISH STOCK* ·

Fish stock may be kept in the refrigerator for 2 days or frozen until required.

MAKES ABOUT 1.1 LITRES (2 PINTS)

450 g (1 lb) fish trimmings
1 leek
2 carrots
1 celery stick
few sprigs of fresh thyme
few sprigs of parsley

1 bay leaf
salt
few black peppercorns
150 ml (¼ pint) dry white wine
   (optional)

·

1 WASH the fish trimmings thoroughly, cut into small pieces and put into a large bowl.

·

2 FINELY chop the leek, carrots and celery and add to the fish trimmings with the thyme, parsley and bay leaf. Pour over 1.1 litres (2 pints) cold water, cover and cook on HIGH for 10–12 minutes or until boiling.

·

3 REMOVE any scum, then re-cover and cook on HIGH for 5 minutes. Add the remaining ingredients and continue to cook on MEDIUM for 15 minutes.

·

4 STRAIN the stock through a colander or a sieve, discarding the solids. Leave to cool, then adjust the seasoning if necessary. Store in the refrigerator and use as required.

· *AIOLI* ·

Aioli is a thick strong garlic mayonnaise, traditionally served with French fish dishes such as Bouillabaise and La Bourride (see pages 107/108)

MAKES ABOUT 300 ML (½ PINT)

4 garlic cloves, skinned
1.25 ml (¼ tsp) salt
2 egg yolks

300 ml (½ pint) olive oil
30 ml (2 tbsp) lemon juice
freshly ground pepper

·

1 CRUSH the garlic cloves to a smooth paste with the salt in a mortar or bowl. Add the egg yolks and beat well with a pestle or spoon. Gradually beat in the oil a drop at a time, until the mixture is thick and smooth.

·

2 WHEN all the oil is added, whisk in the lemon juice. Taste and adjust the seasoning if necessary. Use immediately or store for up to 4 days in a screw-top jar in the refrigerator.

▪ *MAYONNAISE* ▪

The ingredients for mayonnaise should be at room temperature. Never use eggs straight from the refrigerator or the mixture will curdle. If the mixture does curdle it can be rescued by beating the curdled mixture into 5 ml (1 tsp) hot water or lemon juice. When mixture is smooth continue adding the oil.

MAKES 150 ML (¼ PINT)

1 egg yolk
5 ml (1 tsp) Dijon mustard
2.5 ml (½ tsp) salt
1.25 ml (¼ tsp) freshly ground pepper
2.5 ml (½ tsp) granulated sugar

15 ml (1 tbsp) white wine or cider
vinegar or lemon juice
about 150 ml (¼ pint) corn or
groundnut oil

▪

1 PUT the egg yolk into a bowl with the mustard, seasoning, sugar and 5 ml (1 tsp) of the vinegar or lemon juice.

▪

2 MIX thoroughly, then add the oil, drop by drop, whisking continuously add a little extra vinegar or lemon juice if the mixture becomes too stiff to whisk.

▪

3 WHEN all the oil has been added, gradually add the remaining vinegar or lemon juice and mix thoroughly. Use immediately or store for 2–3 weeks in a screw-topped jar in the refrigerator.

THINNING MAYONNAISE If mayonnaise becomes too thick after storage it can be thinned with a little warm water, single cream, vinegar or lemon juice just before serving. Add the extra liquid slowly – too much will spoil the consistency.

VARIATIONS

Different types of mayonnaise can be made by adding the following ingredients to 150 ml (¼ pint) mayonnaise, then leaving it to stand for about 1 hour before serving to allow the flavours to blend.

TARTARE SAUCE 5 ml (1 tsp) chopped fresh tarragon, 10 ml (2 tsp) chopped capers, 10 ml (2 tsp) chopped gherkins, 10 ml (2 tsp) chopped fresh parsley and 15 ml (1 tbsp) tarragon vinegar or lemon juice.

THOUSAND ISLAND MAYONNAISE 15 ml (1 tbsp) chopped stuffed olives, 5 ml (1 tsp) finely chopped onion, 1 chopped hard-boiled egg, 15 ml (1 tbsp) chopped green pepper, 5 ml (1 tsp) chopped fresh parsley and 5 ml (1 tsp) tomato purée.

CUCUMBER MAYONNAISE 30 ml (2 tbsp) finely chopped cucumber.

HERB MAYONNAISE 45 ml (3 tbsp) chopped fresh herbs.

TOMATO MAYONNAISE ½ a tomato, skinned and diced, 1 chopped spring onion and 5 ml (1 tsp) white wine vinegar or lemon juice.

LEMON OR LIME MAYONNAISE finely grated rind of 1 lemon or lime and use lemon or lime juice instead of vinegar.

WATERCRESS MAYONNAISE ¼ bunch of watercress, very finely chopped, to 150 ml (¼ pint) lemon mayonnaise.

· INDEX ·

Ebury Press would like to thank Emma-Lee Gow for her help in the
preparation of this book, and the staff of Richards, Soho, for their advice
and assistance.